God... His Way is Perfect

ADOLPHUS KOOTENAY

Kootenay, Adolphus

GOD... HIS WAY IS PERFECT

Published by: Mary Ann Kootenay
mkootenay66@gmail.com

ISBN 978-1-897544-79-2

PUBLICATION ASSISTANCE AND
DIGITAL PRINTING IN CANADA BY

TABLE OF CONTENTS

GOD'S WORD IS FINAL

Remember, the Bible says,

> *"And if Satan cast out Satan, he is divided against himself; how shall then his kingdom stand?"*[1]

During the time before I came to Christ, on occasion we used to have fierce battles jockeying for recognition we called it "medicine wars". Medicine men and medicine women warred against one another in spiritual warfare. We wanted people to say, "That medicine man or that medicine woman has more power." Eventually one side looked like it prevailed over the other and looked superior.

At the beginning of the ministry that God gave me, which like Paul, I didn't wait to learn in Bible colleges and schools, because I already knew about the spirit world very well. The Holy Spirit guided me on what Scriptures this warfare applied to. No one at that time disclosed the spiritual activities that go on in the Indian religion like I did. I know why it was – because of fear. I just blindly threw myself in the midst of these already-established ministers. I started preaching against the lies of the Indian religion, and I was naïve about the hidden corruption that goes on in Christian circles.

After I got saved I looked at this scenario and questioned, 'How could people ruled by unclean spirits defeat one another?' This meant the devil was only playing around

---

[1] Matthew 12:26

shifting things causing confusion. No one was a winner. They were all still in the same arena but they were blinded by their traditions and beliefs.

THREE STRIKES AGAINST ME

Strike One: The Europeans came to our great country with their spiritual leaders that brought the Holy Bible and perverted it to their own benefit and used it to torment, oppress and kill my ancestors. It isn't until this last century after we knew how to read and write that we finally found out the truth about what the Holy Bible is for. By then the Europeans caused such hatred, anger, vengeance, militancy and murder in the hearts of our host people of this land. The host people blocked off anything that has to do with the White Man, even as an Indian which the White Man call us Red People, we have an enormous struggle as born-again Christians to get through to our own people. They think we are brainwashed by the White Man just as how they were forced to succumb to the demands and exploitation they used in bringing into captivity of our people into the White Man's structure of living.

I had been forced to defend the Bible on many occasions that it's not only a White Man's religion. God meant it for everyone that would listen. The Bible is freedom from the bondage of this world. If it were meant for only the White Man, then God would have kept it hidden from everyone except the White Man. But the Bible states in John

> *"that God so loved the world that He gave His only begotten Son".*[2]

[2] John 3:16

That means the entire world -- every race that lives upon this earth.

I remember when I first got saved, healed and delivered, at the beginning of my walk with God, I was attacked by medicine men that knew me saying that I was hired by the Government to destroy the medicine wheel of the Indian people, and I used to say, "Yes, I was sent by the government," because the Bible again states that in Isaiah,

> *"He will carry the government upon his shoulder."*[3]

When the medicine man accused me of being brainwashed by the White Man's religion, again I would say, "Yes, brainwashed by the blood of the Lamb," although they never understood what I meant. I told the truth. Although in the beginning it was meant for the Israelites, the Hebrew children, once again the Word of the Bible states in John,

> *"He came unto His own and His own received him not. But as many received Him, to them gave He power to become the sons of God, even to them that believe on His name."*[4]

Strike Two: The Holy Bible is written in English. Because of this, my people, the host people, the Indians as they are known in North America, don't trust the Bible at all. They are suspicious, very skeptical even of us. They think the born again Indian is another propaganda from the Government to trick them into another form of captivity.

I heard them say many times in our gatherings before I was saved (when the subject of religion was brought up), "In the forefront was the White Man's spiritual leaders with their crosses and Bibles with long, black robes to beguile us into signing treaties. Now look at what they did to us. They

---

[3] Isaiah 9:6

[4] John 1:11-12

lied and never kept their word and honoured not what they said they would do for us in exchange for this land that the Great Spirit had given us. We trusted their spiritual leaders with their crosses and Bibles. How can we ever trust them again?"

If those supposedly elected spiritual leaders and their churches could do so much damage, unjust and dishonor to the host people of this land, how does anyone expect the host people of this land to trust the general white public?

With all that against me, I have to tell my people the truth about what is actually written in the Bible, not what the White Man first showed. This is why my people think I am brainwashed by the White Man and that I am against them, especially me coming out of the Indian religion and telling my people that the Indian religion is not the truth, although there is a lot of spiritual activity in the Indian religion. These spirits keep us away from receiving the salvation that God put upon this earth through the death of His Son Jesus Christ which is the Indian's God also. The Indians don't realize that Jesus Christ was the Creator of Heaven and Earth. In John, the Bible states,

> *"In the beginning was the Word (Jesus), and the Word (Jesus) was with God, and the Word (Jesus) was God. The same was in the beginning with God. 3All things were made by Him (Jesus); and without Him (Jesus) was not any thing made that was made."*[5]

Strike Three: Again the medicine men and medicine women tell us, "LOOK!" They would point their fingers at pictures made of Jesus Christ and they would say he's got long, blonde hair with blue eyes. Do you see an Indian in that picture? He's a White Man, He's a White Man's god, He has no part with us and plus He's dead. The White Man

[5] John 1:1-3

worship a man dead hanging on a cross." If you are just looking at the outward appearance from a standpoint of not knowing the Scriptures, that's exactly what you perceive – a dead man on a cross, not realizing He rose from the dead and destroyed sin for as many as receive Him.

I was lying awake early one morning around 4 a.m., pondering on the subject of what I have written here on "Three Strikes Against Me", on how the White Man has no conscience, guilt or understanding of what terrible harm they have done to our people, the host people of this land, that our people are waiting for their promises in the treaties signed by two great nations – the White Man and the host people of this great and beautiful land.

The Indian people and this great and beautiful land are slowly being destroyed by the White Man without batting an eye to honor what my people and they agreed upon. I was crying out to God, 'This land is sick, it has cancer, it's going to die. It's been polluted and contaminated. It's never going to recover. Where is the exchange that the White Man promised?'

I cried, and I heard this still, small voice say,

> *"Why are you host people of this land crying, 'Foul, foul!' What is the matter with you anyway? Look in 1 Corinthians 3:19."*

So I jumped out of bed and went into the washroom where the lights were on. I didn't want to wake up my wife by turning the bedroom lights on, and I have all I need in the washroom – the Bible, the concordance, and the dictionary. So I quickly started turning the pages of the Bible until I found 1 Corinthians 3,

> *"For the wisdom of this world is foolishness with God. For it is written, 'He taketh the wise in their*

> *own craftiness.' And again, 'The Lord knoweth the thoughts of the wise, that they are vain."*[6]

Yes, this was so true. The treaty that was signed by our great leaders of that day could never be replaced. They are all dead and gone, but their signatures are still there. No authority could sign over them. The law calls it fraud. So when the White Man saw what bondage they had put themselves with insurmountable wealth all around them.

You see, according to history, it was the Queen of England who begged the Indians if they could use some of our land to sustain their livelihood that was not much in the beginning. Trees to build their homes, land to grow crops, water for their livestock, but, all of a sudden the White Man saw the endless wealth that could be had which started the devices they set up to steal this wealth they envisioned.

Behind closed doors without the knowledge or input of the host people they wrote up the Indian Act and they kept revising it to their benefit as time went on. During that time there were many atrocities done to the host people that caused the rebellion that still goes on today.

Underneath this pile of Indian Acts is the true treaties buried and what the White Man had done to the Indian is never taught in schools. So today no White Man understands why the Indians are crying, "Foul, shame on you White people. We want what was promised by your ancestors in the treaties."

And the White people are saying, "What are you talking about?" because they have no knowledge of what took place at the signing of treaties. The White Man will all stand before God to account for what they did.

"*Vengeance is mine*[7]," saith the Lord God Almighty, and also "*that sin will have you found out*[8]." Now, the technology

---

[6] 1 Corinthians 19-20

[7] Romans 12:19; Hebrews 10:30

[8] Numbers 32:23

that the White Man built beyond human imagination is foolishness to God because it all leads back to square one. And in return for all of this foolishness, the White Man abandoned eternal life and the Bible, and they have dropped it in the hands of the Indian people. Hallelujah! If the Lord doesn't shorten the days9, the White Man will destroy themselves due to their own disobedience to God.

God spoke to me, "Can't you see what they have done? The White Man doesn't know this, but they brought My Word in exchange for what they stole from the Indian people." What God was saying to me was that the White Man brought to us, the host people of this great land of ours, the Good News. Although the White Man misrepresented it, still, The Way, The Truth and The Life, was inside "the Book that the White Man brought over", as the Indians call it, meaning the Holy Bible. It is priceless, it is worth is much more than the promises that was written down at the treaties that were made. What God was saying to me is, "What more can we ask for?" We have it all. God said in Matthew,

> *"But seek ye first the kingdom of God, and his righteousness: and all these things shall be added unto you." He was saying to me, "Forget the government. Look unto me and I will give it."*[10]

Then He told me to turn to Isaiah 51:4-6,

> *"Hearken unto Me, My people; and give ear unto me, O my nation: for a law shall proceed from Me, and I will make My judgment to rest for a light of the people. 5My righteousness is near; my salvation is gone forth, and mine arms shall judge the people; the isles shall wait upon me,*

[9] Mark 13:20
[10] Matthew 6:33

and on mine arm shall they rest. 6Lift up your eyes to the heavens, and look upon the earth beneath for the heavens shall vanish away like smoke and the earth shall wax old like a garment, and they that dwell therein shall die in like manner: but my salvation shall be forever, and my righteousness shall not be abolished."

By this time I was full of the Holy Ghost and I just couldn't contain myself. I woke up my wife to tell her about the revelation that God gave me, and we had a big discussion on the vanity of this world.

CULTURE DEFINED

When trying to explain the differences between tradition and culture, religion and culture enters in also. It is very complex when I consider the ways that my ancestors lived in order to survive.

Many people are confused when speaking about traditions and cultures. In fact, most of the time the Christian Indians are using those terms in the wrong way with the wrong meaning and context.

They seem to think that traditions are the religious part of the Indian when tradition actually is the inherited way of handing down information, opinions, beliefs and customs.

Religion is the awareness of supernatural powers or influences controlling one's life.

Culture is a combination of all of the customary beliefs of a racial, religious or social group, where the custom is the practice of a group of individuals.

So what that means is most Indian people are referring to customs when they mention traditions.

In all of the years I have ministered the gospel to my Indian people, I noticed that the Indian Christians use the term "traditionalists", meaning the unsaved Indians that practice the Indian religion. That ties in all aspects of Mother Earth and animal life as spirits.

There is a great confusion to everyone, because not all who hunt, fish and perform all cultural ways are traditionalists or are into Indian religion. Anyone who practices cultural things does not have to be into Indian religion. Most First

Nations people that I know practice hunting, fishing, etc. Culture has deeply woven Indian religion into it, so that it seems as one – one way of living, one thought, "you can't have one without the other" aspect, etc.

I still very much enjoy hunting, and fishing. In the beginning of my walk with Christ, there was still money in trapping around this area, so I did some trapping every chance I got, and I really enjoyed it. I know many of my brothers in Christ in the north still do a lot of trapping, especially hunting and fishing. Not only non-Christian First Nations people are involved in hunting, fishing and trapping.

Because my ancestors knew of nothing other than what was passed down to them for spiritual beliefs, blinded by spiritual activities thought to be from God, they based their honor and glory on what was taught to them. Sometime when I looked back on stories Mom told me, I got confused on how God was portrayed, she would mention God as the Creator, yet He was never honored as the Most High God. He was always left out. They told stories like God left, He is somewhere else but left behind all His creation for us to use, and that we pleased God when we used and honored His creation.

Another thing I'd like to add is the fact that the enemy is so subtle and crafty. He infiltrated into God's domain when he was in the Garden of Eden. If he can do that, what's holding him back from being in the aisles, pews and pulpits of our churches? Nothing! If we can't keep him out with the knowledge we profess to have with God's Word, what chance did my ancestors have?

CULTURE OVERLAPS TRADITION

Hunting big game is one of many important ways of survival that is a culture. This was how my ancestors survived throughout their lives. There are so many good things that are done in one kill alone, especially in the old days. Because they lived in the wild, they never had the comforts we have today. They had to go without food for days. By the time a hunter got his game, he was near exhaustion because he had to track down his game. At times it took days of walking before they caught up to the game that they were tracking and shot it. Most times it took only one shot to kill game. They had to be very skillful at what they were doing; especially their guns were well taken care of. It was a very delicate piece of commodity that was highly respected to a point where it was priceless in the hand of the owner. Only the owner knew just precisely how the gun worked. The sights were set to the owner's knowledge of the gun; the trigger filed to the owner's touch not to jerk the rifle when the trigger was pulled. They never had the convenience of having a gun belt full of shells like we do nowadays. Sometimes, my dad told me, all they had was one shell that meant life or starvation, so they had to be extremely skilled and have a lot of pride came along with these skills. People talked about the skills that you had, and the people regarded and respected you for what you had. They depended on a person with such skills in time of great need.

There have been many stories told of such men that brought life to a band of Indians near starvation. At the time these historical events took place, there were hardly any settlements. In the northern area of our great province of Alberta, it was bush, lakes, streams and rivers, so it was hard times for my ancestors to even get those shells for their guns. That was why those shells were so precious. And the other thing I mentioned was that nothing was wasted in an animal that was killed for sustenance.

For instance, let's take the moose that is our main source of meat. Every part of the animal that was edible was eaten right to the marrow, the hoof and also all of the insides. They made good use of every part. They made thread out of the sinew, needles out of the heel bone of the moose. They made buckskin out of the hide. Even the thin layer next to the hide was scraped off and dried and eaten. The head was also cooked. The hair on top of the shoulders were taken out and dyed to make designs on coats, vests, gloves, moccasins that they made after the hide was done.

Now, I want to talk about the overlapping of this culture into the religion (the Indian spirituality). I mentioned in my first book of the superstition connected to hunting. My mom used to tell me how they had to rely on the spirit world when the skill of tracking couldn't do it. It was only when they had no alternative but to turn to what she called grandfathers (spirit guides) to do the hunter's job, although the hunter was still needed to shoot the game. Spirits were used to guide the animals to the hunter. There was always a price to pay. The devil made sure that sacrifices and offerings were given unto him through ceremonies and rituals. My ancestors were always kept in darkness by fear. They were afraid to trespass the rules of the enemy, afraid of the threat of losing a loved one.

Sometimes I just don't understand how my forefathers could get so mixed up, but, again I was, too, before I met the Lord Jesus. I took their word for it, and I did what I was taught to do, believing these spirits were sent by God Almighty. It seemed each spirit had a demand of its own, and we followed what these spirits told us to do.

The devil has infiltrated into every good thing. He has not left anything alone that has been regarded as good. As I try to define culture away from religion, I find that the devil had his hand in the culture just as he does in religion. He twists God's Word in such a subtle way, and if we are not watchful we can easily overlook, e.g., the three wise men[11] – it doesn't say that in the Bible -- it says wise men. Or the apple in the garden – where does it say apple? It says fruit.[12] Or money – it says the love of money is the root of all evil, not just having money.[13]

A lot of First Nations people will probably attest to what I am about to write down here. It doesn't take much to offend a First Nations person. Because of this, there are some things you have to be aware of. I mentioned this before but I'll mention it again. Stories told to me by my mom and others – for example, if a trapper, hunter or a fisherman gets more than what is reasonable to man, then this suspicion kicks in. The people will think that this is not pure luck. This person is backed by supernatural forces. He is using good luck medicines through witchcraft. This happens especially when people around this person are frustrated, been hit hard by unsuccessful attempts in getting anything.

I recall one such incident, but the difference was this man was supposed to be a brother in Christ. This was a time when I was sitting under an evangelist from Manitoba. This minister stayed in Alberta for many years ministering around this province. This minister and I were visiting this brother who happened to be trapping forbearing animals that winter. But, he wasn't catching anything in his traps,

---

[11] Matthew 2:1-2

[12] Genesis 3:2-3

[13] 1 Timothy 6:10

and it seemed that all the non-Christians were getting plenty in their traps.

He was at the end of his rope, and he was ready to return to his old way of the Indian religion. He was already collecting medicines to spiritually attack the non-Christians whom he referred to as enemies whom spoke a curse upon his trapline. This brother disclosed this after we spent most of the day at his home. He took us to the back of his house to show us what he had accumulated so far for medicines he had what he collected in a tobacco can hidden under a pile of old lumber.

This was done after we talked him into dropping his plan to return to Indian religion. We helped him burn these so-called Indian medicines. We admonished the brother of the possibility of opening himself up to the enemy, and he'd be a lot worse than he is now. After all of this, we got together and prayed. We even got him to a point where he confessed his wrong intentions to God. We asked the Lord to break all the curses upon him and his trapline.

What I am trying to expose is the fact that sort of spiritual activities still goes on today, and it's rapidly gaining all sorts of power. Many of the young medicine men are actually going into deeper spiritual practices trying to find powers beyond our ancestors. I've ministered in areas where fishing, trapping and hunting were still done for survival. I witnessed first hand what these curses could do throughout generations of practice because I ran into a lot of evidence on people when I was ministering in northern Manitoba. I spent approximately ten days in a fishing community where we had church every night, plus I made home visits during the day praying for people that had curses upon them from years of medicine wars. God did a mighty work among those people with curses.

It seems that even in Christianity you have to constantly pray off these curses. It sure looks like it's going to be there whether you are a born-again Christian or not. This is exactly the same as the stumbling blocks and snares he sets out for us daily.

My mom told me stories about the times they almost died of starvation. No one in her family could get game. They would go out every day with barely enough strength, hoping that somehow they would get their game.

Some of the hunters were so weak they couldn't even go out any more. It was in times like these they had no alternative but to resort to the medicine men or medicine women for help, and it seemed to work.

But looking at these stories of hard times today from a born-again Christian's view, it was God who intervened for them to get their game, not the medicine men or medicine women, not the spirits that were called on for help.

Hold it! Let's have another look at this, because sometimes the devil will also make things happen to strengthen his stronghold. This is probably where all of this confusion comes from. The enemy could also do this to keep our people in bondage. If my Indian people knew God, they could have come out of this bondage long ago.

In the Bible it says,

> *"because the devil cometh not, but for to steal and to kill, and to destroy."*[14]

The devil has no mercy. He was going to kill them all by starving them. The battle of good and evil took place. The good won, but it was never recognized. The evil got the glory to keep the naïve and the non-Christian in bondage, to keep them believing that it was the medicine man or the medicine women and their spiritual powers. The people would say, "If it wasn't for the medicine men or medicine women with their spirits we would have died of starvation." In this way the people looked up to man and the devil stole God's glory.

---

[14] John 10:10

But it is so wonderful to have such a loving and unconditional God. He loved the world so much that He gave His Son to die for us so as we can be with Him someday. This is why the Word of God says He will never leave nor forsake us. This is why I got my chance to finish what I had in my mind to do in finishing these two books.

He never left me even when I completely shamed His Word when I fell into alcohol (written in my first book). He gave me another chance to redeem myself after falling to the lies of the devil. My parents were also deceived and lived a long life of darkness, yet in the end my mom came to the Lord, although my dad died before I was saved. Still the man who raised me whom I thought was my dad received the Lord. He is now 93 years old.

I can still remember that day that my late wife and I led him to the Lord while he was on his deathbed in a hospital in Edmonton, the capital city of Alberta, Canada. He was brought down by years of alcohol consumption, and his whole body was infected by a rash that caused his skin to fall off. He was lying on a sheet of wax paper that had some sort of Vaseline-type of salve so that his body wouldn't stick to it. His whole body had salve on it and only a thin sheet covered his naked body. He was in a fetal position, and all he made was a painful sound of agony as he breathed very rapidly.

I remember his telling me if he makes it through this one, he was going to quit his drinking. That was right after I led him to the Lord and a miracle took place. His body dried up and he was healed within a couple of days. Within five days from the day he accepted the Lord, he left the hospital fully healed. He drank all of his life up to that point, and he has stopped drinking since then. Without rehabilitation of any kind – just the touch of the Holy Spirit completely took that craving and desire away. This happened around 1994 and he is still not drinking today. He still takes good care of himself and he lives by himself. Also he has a sound mind, and he is able to take a long walk uptown where he lives. God really has blessed him.

The Unexplained Moose Kill

While I was heavily involved in the practices of the Indian religion, my late wife and I had the opportunity to do some hunting for a Métis medicine man that we did sweat lodges with. He said that his body was craving for moose meat and the insides of a moose that we First Nations people consider a delicacy. He asked us if we could go out and get a moose for him. He indicated that he would help us out on this hunt. So the next day my late wife and I went west around what the people call Whitecourt Forest where we hunted and trapped most of our younger days.

We usually try road hunting first before we go on foot, so we decided to make a big loop on oil roads once we got there. We hit every nook and cranny of trails off the main route that we were going. We didn't see hide or hair of any game. Usually we would see plenty of game on these roads that we were taking. But this day, nothing. We were very disappointed and we couldn't understand this luck we were having. It was already getting late towards noon, and we had been on the road since 5 a.m. We left home while it was still dark, and we were hoping that we'd get our game while the game was still feeding along the roads in the early morning hours.

Finally, we were only a couple of miles away from the blacktop where we were going to end our road hunting expedition. From there we were going to decide where we were going to start our foot hunting. All of a sudden from this cut bank along the road where the road builders took down a hill came this moose in full flight slipping and sliding with its tongue hanging out. You can tell it's been running for a while especially when his tongue hung out like that.

I had all four wheels on my truck locked with the truck skidding. I was trying to stop so that I can at least get one shot off before the moose crosses the road on the opening along the road. But the moose just came to a stop and stood still there in the middle of the road, giving me ample time to jump off the truck, to undo the safety on the gun, aim and fire.

I could tell the moose was hit hard by the way it hunched its shoulders, so I didn't take another shot. I just watched it slowly walk off the road into this muskeg. It lay down, rolled on its back and started kicking and died.

Oh my, it couldn't have dropped in a cleaner place. The moose was lying among grass and moss with a little water, just ideal for dressing a moose.

I found out what the old man meant when he said, 'I'll help you out,' when we got his moose and all of the insides back to his place. I was expecting him to pull out his wallet and offer to pay for the gas and the kill, which, if and a big "IF", I took any, it would have been just probably for the gas and nothing else.

The words he used confused me. I should have known better. Anyway I completely misunderstood what he meant. I found out that he was talking about a spiritual intervention, not finances.

I sort of wondered what it was that the moose was running from – what was chasing the moose to be that exhausted when it came onto the road and suddenly stopped. A moose running from something doesn't stop and wait to be shot at. All I should have seen was dark hair and legs of an animal crossing the road at a tremendous speed. There is no way a moose will stop for anything if a predator was on its tail.

It must have shown by my body language to the old man that I was expecting something. We were just standing around when the old man asked me, "How did you get the moose?"

I was all excited telling him, how strange of an incident took place getting that moose, like something was pre-arranged to happen this way. The old man just smiled and said, "*hi, hi,*" (meaning "thank you" in Cree), and I knew he sure wasn't thanking me when he said that. Just in case you are wondering, he was thanking the grandfathers (spirit guides). It was only then did I realize what he had done.

My forefathers practiced as this old man did, and this religious belief has such a stronghold in the past up until today. In explaining what I have witnessed about overlapping, this is as close as I can come for those to understand culture versus religion.

While backtracking and reminiscing on stories and experiences that happened during hunting, trapping and fishing, it seems that superstition and curses somehow played a big part. If you are having bad luck in any of these three areas, you would blame it on envy or jealousy of some person, and you would retaliate by using what we call Indian medicines that don't do a thing for you. If it is a curse, then it's spiritual, done by the devil. Like I said in my first book, these roots and plants are tangible. They don't fly around by themselves. The only way it can fly is if it's transported by the devil or to throw it like you would throw a ball. Other than that, they are just roots and plants. It's the unclean spirits that do the deceiving.

God made the roots and plants, not the devil. But the devil infiltrated its own powers to exploit the naïve and non-Christian to control their minds in thinking that these roots and plants are spiritual.

My ancestors on both sides of my parents passed down this belief that all plant life was spiritual, which in turn was passed down to me. The devil used it to his advantage until I was converted to Jesus Christ.

OLD THINGS MUST PASS AWAY

In the days of my grandfather and my grandmother even during my mom and dad's days, there was nothing to compare to what they were doing – I mean Scripture-wise. They were considered pagans because of what they worshipped in those days. The only thing they could compare it with was their mistakes they made during their survival, such as hunting, fishing, trapping, etc. Come to think of it, even in our generation, there was no such thing as a Born Again Christian. It was unheard of. The only other religion besides our own was the Roman Catholic faith. We never understood it like our Indian religion. Plus, we were nomadic people. There was a wild, free spirit in our blood. Our people tried to stay isolated. They seemed to feel a sense a freedom when they were out in nowhere land among wild game. That was why there were very few people residing on our reservations. The reservations were just a gathering place in between their hunting grounds. All we ever knew was the traditional ways, nothing to

rightly divide the Scriptures[15]

Rightly dividing the truth, there must have been a lot of miracles done by God that was never recognized. They couldn't connect it with God because our people walked by sight. This made it so easy for the enemy, the devil, to infiltrate and steer our people away from the truth.

---

[15] 2 Timothy 2:15

So many times I defended God Almighty because so many of my people, especially relatives, seemed to think our forefathers were the ones that brought us through the hard, desperate, almost genocidal situations in past times. They would say, "If it wasn't for our grandfather's strength, we would never be here." They would give credit to our forefathers. I would counter with the Word, "If God didn't love the world so much, we wouldn't be here!" God keeps giving us chance after chance after chance to turn to Him. But our forefather's teaching of the spirit world gets in God's way. That goes with other religions.

> *Be not deceived. God is not mocked. For whatever a man soweth, that shall he also reap.*[16]

What does that mean? How you bring up your children – what religion, no religion, whatever belief you teach them – to steal and lie, work hard, being lazy, etc. That is exactly what they are going to grow up being. When you are conditioned in certain things, sometimes only God could break through that conditioning.

Example: When I was just a kid, I heard of this city in southern Alberta. Our people from here went working picking sugar beets from here. Years later I was looking over the map of Alberta. I decided to look at these places where some of my relatives worked. I came across this city that I heard of all of my young days. I said to myself, "Whoever made this map spelled this city wrong." I was positively sure they called this city "Leftbridge", not "Lethbridge". I am putting down this example because of how our minds work, or what a person may think he/she thought was heard and misinterpret its meaning.

This is how easy a person can be deceived. What I am saying is what chance did our ancestors have against the

[16] Galatians 6:7

devil? Even today after knowing the Scriptures we still have a huge problem with the devil. This is why

The old things must pass away. We become a new creature in Christ

I am talking about the devil that had a stronghold on my ancestors. He used signs and lying wonders to keep my people, the Indians, in bondage. We have to stay in the Word and walk by the Word to have a good chance of overcoming what the devil lay before us as a trap.

Regardless of what situation my forefathers were in, the enemy always had a part. My ancestors never knew it was the devil. They always thought it was God that they spiritually corresponded with, not knowing the enemy also had spiritual powers used only to beguile people with. Why I say this is because I was always told it was God who had given us these powers to communicate with the spirit world. When I first encountered with these manifestations, the elders (medicine men/women) told me not to fear. It is God using these spirits as messengers. I always took it as such until my conversion to Christ. This is why I said in the first book that I had so many questions that needed to be answered, and only God could answer through His Word. The ministers of the gospel cannot answer me, although they themselves used the same Scriptures. They applied it only in a context that they knew about. These ministers never encountered the manifestation of a spirit in animal form, or a fowl, or the creeping things that spoke to them with an audible voice. In this same way, in the Garden of Eden, the devil spoke to Eve.

Right to this very hour, the devil is still on his quest

to kill, steal and destroy.

I never could understand my Christian Indian brothers and sisters. They have so many questions. For instance, what I am now writing is because they wondered about the natural things that go on. I also know where they are coming from because of the residential school experience and the government's social programs. A lot of them were wards of the government such as through adoption. Many ended up in White Christian homes.

When they became of age, they found an identity problem. They go searching for their roots, and they find it on a reservation somewhere where the culture is totally different than what they are used to. Some stay away from ever interacting with their lost relatives and most try to restart their Indian heritage by going into the traditions of the ancestral spirituality. The ones that stay in Christianity taught by the White people tend to have a lot of questions and I notice they want to be part of their Indian roots but just how far is too far.

They seem to be feeling around and they ask such questions as, "What is wrong with making moccasins out of animal hides?" It all depends on what purpose was it for, and who is making these moccasins (dances, some older Indians, who shot the wild game, were they traditional Indian people)? Where did the hide come from? Was it done by traditional Indian people? Where everything they get has a spiritual meaning, where the spirit world is honored. Like I've been saying, the devil seems to have his hand into everything.

I know what I used to do before I was saved. I honored my grandfathers (spirit guides or mediums) for the kill, all the animal delicacy were set aside for a special presentation to our dead forefathers who loved hunting at a feast specially prepared for them and the spirit world. This delicacy of animal were secretly guarded, put away and only taken out when the time for the feast comes around. No matter what situation you are in, such as near starvation, it cannot be used. You would rather starve than use it for yourself. That's how strict it can get when you are under the bondage of the spirit world. One small error can cause you huge repercussions.

One time a young lady was told to hang offerings to the grandfathers, which she did. Something terrible happened in the immediate family – a tragedy involving a vehicle accident. Many of her family were seriously injured and one lost a life. They couldn't understand why. One thing they concluded was the fact it was a spiritual incident. But "where did they do wrong?" was the question.

One of them decided to consult a medicine woman who was a medium. When the answer came back, they were astonished to find the answer to be how they put up their last offering that was done by the young lady. She got her instruction mixed up. She was to go to the lodge where a ritual was done, to go inside the lodge and tie the print offerings like a necktie. The tie was supposed to be facing west but she tied the offerings from the outside of the structure facing east. That's the strictness I was talking about. Everything has to be done precisely as instructed.

That is why I said fear was the enemy's main weapon. He controls by fear. He is obligated to enforce his rule or he would lose his control. There are so many questionable items that I just stay clear of. There are a lot of Indian crafts that are so beautifully made. Sometimes I desire something to use for appearance sake but, like I said, it's too risky. Not risky for yourself only, but it may create doubt and as a stumbling block to others who are weak. "What about sweet grass?" is another question that is frequently asked. They never seem to go to God for the answers. If it is causing your spirit to questions these things, it must not be any good. Sweet grass is incense.

What does God say about incense?

Incense is an abomination to me[17]

---

[17] Isaiah 1:13

Indian Christians seem to be bound and determined to put themselves in jeopardy by means of disobeying God's authority for purposely overlooking passages pertaining to a subject at hand. Why do I say this? I will reiterate, "If I can do it, you can also." I mean to completely restrain myself from ever dabbling in anything pertaining to the Indian beliefs and ways. I've walked without it like the apostle Paul did, and I did just fine. I pray that someday that I will have an opportunity to repeat the apostle Paul's words:

> *For I am now ready to be offered and the time of my departure is at hand, I have fought the good fight, I have finished my course, I have kept the faith; Henceforth there is laid up for me a crown of righteousness, which the Lord, the righteous Judge shave give me at that day.*[18]

---

[18] 2 Timothy 4:6-8

THE DEVIL IS A LIAR

I could never forget the first time I got to minister. It was in a huge church and it was full to capacity. It was in the city of Edmonton, Alberta, Canada. I knew without a doubt on how controversial my testimony was. It really offended those that follow the spiritual beliefs of the Indian religion, but still, I had to tell the truth of what Jesus Christ did in my life. I wouldn't be alive if it wasn't for Jesus Christ. But, I tell you, it wasn't easy. Everything hit me all at once. When I entered that huge building, especially when I got inside the sanctuary and I saw all of the Indian people in the congregation. There were even some of the Indian men sitting there among the crowd with long braids on.

Oh, I tell you, the devil hit me on all sides. He started whispering in my ear telling me, "You see those Indians with long braids? Well, they came here not to listen but to kill you. If they get near you, they are going to knife you. So all you have to do is not tell your testimony, preach on something else and they will leave you alone."

Anyway I sat down in the front row because the pastor was going to allow me to minister that night. All the while that I was waiting I never got a minute's rest from the devil. He kept taunting me relentlessly right up to the time I was called up. I felt like running out of that church because the pressure was immense and fear continuously tried to enter, but I also kept my mind on Jesus.

I also whispered, 'Jesus' over and over. I also vividly remember exactly how I started my sermon. I quoted

Genesis 3:1 "Now the serpent was more subtle than any beast of the field which the Lord God had made." I got to tell all of my testimony along with Scripture to back it up.

This Scripture was the beginning of how all religions got started and also when the devil took over the world system. This was also the introduction to my testimony, because that's when the devil used an animal to speak to Eve, just like he does in our healing lodges when he manifests himself in whatever form of the animal kingdom. It depends on what we as Indians honor as our spirit guide or grandfathers. If it is the buffalo, that is exactly how he will sound, like the clacking of hooves on the rocks, the blowing through the nostrils, and the grunting. You would swear there was a buffalo walking around on those heated rocks.

Now when these spirits manifest as a bear, you not only hear the sounds the bear makes, it would start walking around visiting each person that is sitting in a circle around the heated rocks. The bear is usually small like a newborn cub. We are sitting on our knees and it seemed to be as tall as us when it is standing on its hind legs. I recall the times it put its paws one on each side of my shoulders and started poking its nose on my head, kind of blowing and sniffing on my head and on my chest area, like searching to detect if any curses or sickness is in that area of my body.

I've also witnessed where the spirit manifested itself as the thunderbird (eagle). It would flap its wings around. It is stationary but turning round and round. The tip of its wings would hit you in the head several times throughout the times it is going around. Then it stops. You could hear its talons scratching the water pail like it is balancing itself on the pail. Then it would splash water on the heated rocks with its wing.

Another time while camping out in the wilderness hunting for game, several of us decided to do a sweat lodge all because it was an ideal setting. For one, during the chanting and praying to the grandfathers, the lodge slowly started rocking back and forward and then it shook. Something that sounded like a little bird started flying around. Inside you can hear the small wings when it would hit the ceiling of the lodge. Who knows, it might well have been a bat for all we know. It was pitch dark inside. All you can see is the red hot glow of the heated rocks. It flew around for quite some time and suddenly disappeared just as fast as it came in.

No one said a word about what we heard, all except the one we selected to conduct the lodge. All he said was. "We had a visitation from our grandfathers."

How can a person not believe with all of that spiritual activity going on? What you hear, also what you feel, you cannot doubt. The stronghold gets stronger each time this happens.

When I made the altar call, people that needed prayer and deliverance lined up from wall to wall. Oh man, I tell you, then the anointing of God came down, and the Holy Ghost power started hitting those people that needed deliverance from strongholds of witchcraft, curses, ancestral strongholds started breaking. Then I knew why the devil tried so hard to stop me. He knew that he was going to get evicted from all of the homes (human bodies) that he previously occupied.

The pastor must have been touched deeply on what I disclosed pertaining to the Indian religion. He invited me to be a guest on a radio talk show that he had as part of his ministry. That night he also had another young First Nations man to interview, but I was first in line. After the interview was done, I went out of this little room where we'd been talking. There sat this young First Nations man just outside of the door. He heard every word that we said during this interview. I could see fear in his eyes when I looked at him.

Then he told me, "You shouldn't have said what I heard you say in there. You are talking about dangerous people that won't hesitate to kill, and they have the power to do so. I know of such medicine men/women back from where I come from. I wouldn't dare open my mouth around them to say what you just said."

He proceeded in telling me about this particular medicine man (he even named the man) who would astral travel during the night and randomly selected anyone he pleased to kill just anyone he chooses in their sleep. They never wake up.

This fear that this young First Nations man showed toward this medicine man is exactly what keeps the First Nations people in this powerful bondage throughout generations. This fear is also what keeps our First Nations born-again Christians gagged from telling the truth. I have seen many born-again First Nations hem and haw, stutter and cower when they are confronted by their relatives whom are powerful believers in the Indian religion. If we as First Nations born-again Christians show fear when confronted by medicine men/women in front of our children, naturally our children will also have the same problem. Our children hear us shouting praises and saying, "Greater is He that is in me than he that is in the world." When it comes time to prove it, we tremble and cower when we run into the enemy.

I don't mean to start a fisticuffs with our relatives. The Word of God says to use wisdom, as it says

> *"be ye therefore wise as serpents and harmless as doves".*[19]

What we have to do is stand firm with the Word of God and hit them back with the truth. I know how radical they can get but still we have to tell them without succumbing to anger. We have to do this all in love because these are people bound by unclean spirits. It is not the spirits we are

---

[19] Matthew 10:16

telling it to, because the spirits already know who Jesus Christ is.

These people are potential Christians so it all depends on how we as Christians present the Word of God. Don't forget about how early churches misrepresented and totally distorted the Word of God. Because of this, our First Nations people don't want to have anything to do with something that has any kind of a White Man's imprint. Still, we have an all-powerful God and the Word of God states that once His Word goes out, it will never come back void.

It didn't matter to me, because I spoke from what I encountered from years of spiritual bondage. This was what I was talking about. When I mentioned medicine wars, not really realizing that is was the same power, we challenge one another with it to see whose power was superior.

Anyway several years later, to be exact nine years later, we moved from our home on the reservation to Slave Lake to be closer to my daughter who got married around that area. It was during this time in Slave Lake that we had some terrible rainstorms. There were weeks of torrential downpours that caused the creeks, streams and rivers to overflow their banks. It washed out roads and small bridges, flooded homes. It did a lot of damage. I used to read the local newspaper just to be updated in the happenings around our areas.

We were blessed to be living outside of Slave Lake because I read in the paper that half of the town of Slave Lake was under water. It was at this same time I read of a drowning. There are a lot of Indian reservations that they call First Nations around the lake that is called Slave Lake. On one of these reservations just west of where we lived, they found an old First Nations man among some debris that was washed up on higher ground along a river that runs through the reservation. It was believed that the old man tried to escape the flood by wading through the current of this flood. He probably got knocked down by the debris and got swept away.

The one thing that I picked up right away was the name of the old fellow. It was the name of that notorious medicine man that young First Nations man mentioned approximately fifteen years before. I was thinking to myself, 'When are my First Nations people ever going to learn, that this supernatural phenomenon doesn't belong to us? It's only making us think what we do to make fools out of us. When it's done with us, it just discards us and hops unto a younger body to control.' On and on it goes, generation to generation, while the person it just discarded ends up in hell, just like the way it discarded this old man.'

I thought of the time I was one step away from death. I remember still thinking that I had this supernatural power even though I was about to die and had no strength of my own. The devil still kept me thinking that I had this great supernatural power, and just imagine, I would have died thinking that way. I would have gone to hell because I was deceived, and then I had eternal regrets for not knowing the truth while I was still on this earth.

I know it is the unclean spirits that distort our minds to keep us in their bondage until life is gone from out of us. I was one step away from death, yet the demons hung in there in my body as long as my heart was still beating. Maybe it was because I was young. I know the unclean spirits don't have any alternative but to leave an old worn out man. An old body has met its end, and they have no use for it any more. But a young body has still got hope of recovering. The Word of God describes the devil's ways in John:

> *"He was a murderer from the beginning, when he speaketh a lie, he speaketh of his own: for he is a liar, and the father of it."*[20]

---

[20] John 8:44

He lies to us by telling us that we have spiritual powers, a gift given to us by God, that we were born with it. Actually, it is the devil's powers passed down through our parents' bloodline

"visiting the iniquities of our fathers"[21]

because we are blinded by our forefathers' wickedness and disobedience. We could not detect this lie, so we believe his lies. Just like this old man: Where was the power that he thought he had all of his life? When he needed it, why didn't he lift off from that water to dry ground? Because the devil had no more use for him. He was too old and he was ready to die anyway, so he had to be discarded. I am warning you – you that follow Indian religion – don't rely on those signs and wonders. It is a lie. God's Word says,

"Walk by faith, not by sight", Blessed are those that don't see, yet believe"

I am talking from experience, from before I got saved when I followed signs and wonders to today after twenty-six years of following God's Word. I see the difference like night and day.

Don't get me wrong, because there are still signs after you receive Christ into your heart[22], but the difference is that you now know for a fact that these signs come from God Almighty!

It says in the Bible,

"The Lord working with them, and confirming the Word with signs following"[23]

---

[21] Exodus 20:5
[22] Mark 16:17-18
[23] Mark 16:20

Note it says "following", not like what the devil does. The devil makes signs and lying wonders happen ahead of time to make you believe.

The devil lies to us by telling us that we acquired this spiritual gift with all of its powers from God, that we were born with them. It seemed to be in the family tree for generations. Speaking for myself, I was taught from childhood. I watched both of my parents on how they conduct themselves when it came time for a doctoring or doing a ritual, ceremony, unpacking their medicine bag and also performing pipe ceremonies. I just naturally fell into their pattern from years of watching.

They taught me to be careful and to be precise, never to fool around during the time I or someone else is doing any type of spiritual ceremony or whatever the case may be, in honor of the grandfathers (the spirit world). When we obey and do what we are taught step by step, then the enemy is obligated to honor his end by creating what he does best – spiritual manifestations – whatever will cause us to continue believing.

Like this old man who astral traveled and put fear into mankind all of his life. What happened to his power when he needed it most? Why didn't he lift off the water current to high, dry land? It is because the old man never did have his own power to astral travel in the first place. The devil was doing what he did to Jesus in Luke 4:5. Remember Jesus wasn't glorified yet. He was still a human when the devil took Him into a high mountain to show Jesus his kingdom. When the devil was done with this old man, he no longer allowed this old man to use his power. The devil had no use for this old man any more. The old man was feeble and very old, ready to be put in the ground soon anyway. He just let the old man be swept away. In the book John it says,

"The devil came to kill, steal and destroy"[24]

Take this as a warning for you that are bound by Indian religion. Don't get taken in by those sounds, signs and lying wonders. It leads nowhere but into utter darkness.

---

[24] John 10:10

THE CURSE THAT MISSED

There is something that used to cause wonderment and also to scratch my head in trying to figure it out. How could this be? One incident that caused such a concern was my late mother-in-law. She was blind, starting at a very young age in life. She was approximately twelve years old when it happened. This information I received from my late wife and also my mother who used to be a good friend of my late mother-in-law until my late wife and I started staying together.

My mother-in-law accused my mother in using mind control medicines on my late wife so that I could be her husband, which caused their friendship to collapse, although my mom did no such thing. It was love that put us together. It was because my mom was well-known to carry these mind control medicines by many, including my late mother-in-law. This caused my late mother-in-law to believe that this was why my late wife fell in love with me.

The information for what caused my mother-in-law's blindness came from many of the relatives that witnessed the life of my late mother-in-law from childhood. This blindness that happened so suddenly was caused by a curse. What baffled me was the fact that she did nothing to anybody to deserve this kind of punishment. Although many believe, including my mom, that this curse was meant for my late mother-in-law's mother who was a very wicked woman.

She never had anything good to say to anyone. There were always evil curses coming out of her mouth. If she had the chance to kill someone, I am sure nothing would stop her from doing so. My mom once told me a story about this wicked woman.

It was about the time she managed somehow to snare a man as her first husband. There happened to be a big celebration going on at another Indian reservation close by. This man so wanted to take part in this celebration, but this wicked woman would not allow him to leave. She demanded that he stay home with her while everyone else was going over there to have fun.

My mom said they were sitting outside by a campfire probably having tea and some lunch, when the man took out his drum and started to sing an old love song. Right away the wicked woman got very angry thinking that this husband was singing with some other women on his mind that he was probably going to meet at that celebration.

She actually asked her husband, “What woman is that song for? Who are you thinking of?” She grabbed a frying pan and scooped a bunch of ashes and coals from the fire and threw it in her husband’s face.

The hot coals burned out one of her husband’s eyes and it caused it to go blind. According to how the story goes, the husband complained of blindness in one eye. This wicked woman said, “Good for you. Mess with me some more!” She didn’t have any conscience of the terrible harm she’d done to her husband.

When I heard the story of how my mother-in-law got blind at a very young teenager, this question popped in my mind, “How could this curse miss its mark and hit someone else instead?”

Another thing I didn’t take into consideration was the fact this evil deed was from the devil. As you know, there is no such thing as the devil in the Indian religion, which is what caused me to completely leave out the devil. Our belief was about good and evil spirits. We also believed that we as medicine men had good spirits because we were taught to believe these spirits were sent by the Creator. One thing I never realized was the enemy the devil was in control all along. He did whatever was good for him. The more fear he put into our lives, the more power he had to dictate and control us. The devil usually will hit something or someone that would cause more pain and fear. For example, if you had five children, there is always one out of those five children that is special. It holds a special place in your heart. That is the one that the devil will most likely use to insert pain in the lives of that family. He will attack anything you hold dearly to inflict severe pain or extreme trouble in your entire family.

This is what I was trying to explain when I said, "All of the instructions passed down by our ancestors on how to put up offering, what shades of color, how long, how wide, how to put the structure of your lodges, which way it is supposed to face, the whole entire Indian spiritual belief system has to be precise. You can't misplace an offering, or a lodge structure, or anything else you have been taught, or else. There are consequences to pay, such as inflicting pain and suffering. This is how the devil controls, contrary to God's unconditional love. So even though the curse was meant for my late wife's grandmother, it hit her mother instead, because that was going to cause more pain and trouble for the wicked woman.

THE ENEMY KEEPS TRYING

Another time a few years after my conversion, a brother in Christ told me this story about how the devil tried to entice him into making a covenant with him, but when this took place he never knew Jesus Christ. At that time he was a practicing medicine man. As medicine men, we only knew what our ancestors brought from generations of communicating with these spirits, and that is what we followed.

When this spirit asked him for his second oldest son in exchange to unlimited spiritual power, this brother didn't know he was actually talking with the devil. He was in a sweat lodge when this spirit confronted him about that one particular son. His second oldest son was somehow so special to this brother. He had two other sons, but this one he seemed to favor more than the rest, always doing more for him and being overly protective of this son. This little boy went where his daddy went. It would break his heart if something bad ever would happen to this son. This was the son the devil wanted. This spirit told this brother to sleep on this offer. Tomorrow at sundown he would be expecting his answer.

The brother made up his mind long before he even went to bed that night. There was no way he was going to let his son go as an offering for his personal gain. He said that once he made up his mind, he forgot about everything and just went about doing what he generally did.

The next day just after supper he was going out of the house putting tools and stuff away that he had scattered around throughout the day back to their proper places. Then he came in and started watching a program on television when he remembered he didn't padlock his truck toolbox, so he just had to go out one more time. He said the sun was down by then but it was still light outside. He went out the door and left to go along his house when he caught this flash of light at the corner of his eye. He stopped to look.

He said that there used to be a power pole at the back of his house. There on that power pole sat a figure. It looked like an outline of a vulture perched on a tree with his sharp shoulders sticking out. When he stopped and took a closer look, he could see it wasn't a fowl. It looked like a small, skinny person. What looked like shoulders of a vulture were actually the knees of this small black person. When it moved its head, his eyes came like flashes of light, like a diamond in a ring or on a necklace.

Then it spoke with a deep, strong voice. It said, "Have you made up your mind on that proposition I offered you about your son?" He said, "It was only then that I realized that I had never given this spirit the answer. I only made up my mind up to myself. So I said, 'Yes, I did. I decided that you can't have him.' Just then the figure vanished before my eyes. I never ever heard from this spirit again."

THE DREAMCATCHER

So many of my Indian Christian brothers and sisters ask me the same question, "What about the dreamcatcher?" Because they all have them and it makes it a nice decoration for their homes and vehicles and it also looks so harmless to the eyes, it is something that everyone has. It is something to be desired, very appealing to the eye and it's very subtle.

The Bible in Genesis the Bible says,

> *"Now the serpent was more subtle than any beast the Lord had made."*[25]

The devil can use a device that can kill you and make it look harmless to the eye. In 1 John the Bible talks about "*the lust of the eye*"[26]

and also back in Genesis it mentions on how the devil made the fruit to look so attractive to the eye, a fruit to be desired[27], if you look at the root of where the dreamcatcher originated from, you will realize that it came from the spirit world.

The story I received about the dreamcatcher was way before I got saved. It was told to us at substance abuse workshops. At the time it was told to us I was so amazed I said to myself, 'Oh my! Such a gifted person to receive such an honor from the spirit world.'

---

[25] Genesis 3:1

[26] 1 John 2:15-16

[27] Genesis 3:1

The person who told us this said these dreamcatchers are to be hung on the window of your bedroom. It is believed that dreams enter through the windows of your home. The bad dreams and nightmares are caught on the netting on a dreamcatcher. You will find a small round hole in the center of it where the good dreams are let through.

Today these dreamcatchers are sold everywhere. It's a money-making commodity that belongs to the world system run by the devil. In Luke the devil said to Jesus, "*This was given unto me and whomever I give, I give it.*"[28]

God said in Exodus, *"Thou shalt not bow down to it or serve it."*[29]

The devil says in Luke, "*if you bow down to me [or his system] all of this shall be yours.*"[30]

The bottom line? It's a scheme the devil uses in a very subtle way to beguile the world, including Christians that are not watchful, especially the lukewarm ones. The Word of God says that it will fool the very elect if it were possible.

So, in conclusion, look around you and dig around and see what all else you have brought into your life and home inadvertently. The enemy, the devil, uses even your children.

Just recently we did some deliverance on a brother in the Lord who was brought up in Indian religion. After his release from these strongholds, he started noticing little things that he picked up and brought home that were related to his beliefs. Just when we thought he had gathered everything, his little boy who's been watching all along said, "Dad, I have something that I brought home from school, where they are teaching us in making traditional things." He brought out some drumsticks that he had made. They were as small as matchsticks. If he had not shown us, these

---

[28] Luke 4:5

[29] Exodus 20

[30] Luke 4:5

things could have sat unnoticed for years. That's how subtle the enemy is.

Another time a sister in the Lord told me this story of herself on how deceitful the enemy is. She said it started just after a conference she attended for a weekend. We had all made new friends during a time of sharing personal things in their lives. As they were saying their last farewells in hugging one another, one of the women gave her a gift for a memento – a small, beaded hair holder – that she dropped in her leather coat pocket.

In all of the excitement that went on, she completely forgot about it. One day a long time later she noticed a tingling on the tips of her fingers that she passed off as nothing. Later on she started noticing that the tips of her fingers were getting numb. Then again, she thought nothing of it. Then it went up into her fingers and continued going throughout her whole hand and up into her arm. Paralysis was setting in.

One day she was emptying out her coat pocket. There fell the beaded memento that was given her. Right away the Holy Spirit rose up in her as a warning and it all came back to her in a moment of where this came from. All this time this thing was hidden in her pocket, yet somehow the enemy kept it away from view, all the while attacking her. When she realized that it was this thing that was causing the paralysis, she immediately decided to burn up the beaded hair holder. When she did, her paralysis disappeared.

In the Book of Deuteronomy, God said,

> *"The graven images of their gods shall ye burn with fire: thou shalt not desire the silver or gold that is on them, nor take it unto thee, lest thou be snared therein: for it is an abomination [shamefully wicked; a feeling of disgust; hate; loathing] to the Lord thy God. Neither shalt thou bring an abomination into thine house, lest thou*

be a cursed thing like it: and thou shalt utterly abhor [reject] it: for it is a cursed thing."[31]

Now that we have become God's children, we can say "their gods or beliefs." What we were in before the Lord found us we have been separated by Jesus Christ's shed blood on the cross. So by this, we are no longer part of our ancestral beliefs. We are a royal priesthood set aside by God.

[31] Deuteronomy 7:25-26

MARY ANN & THE DREAMCATCHER

The spiritual influence of Indian paraphernalia doesn't just centre on Indians. If a White person is involved entering the medicine wheel, he or she is affected just as bad as an Indian. My wife Mary Ann is White and she is of German/ Russian descent. She always had Indian friends from childhood right to today. She tells me this story in her own words of a gift she received from her best friend who is a Lakota Sioux Indian.

"About one year after I was saved, I went to visit my friend who is a Lakota Sioux Indian. She and I have been friends since we were 12 years old, so I trusted my dear friend. She called me "kola" (a Lakota Sioux word for "a very close friend"). My friend wanted to give me a gift, so she gave me a key ring dream catcher with red leather fringes. It looked so nice, and I treasured it, especially since it came from her.

I took it home and my 16-year-old daughter saw the gift, and she grabbed it out of my hand. I said, "Come on, give it back! That came from my friend." My daughter wouldn't give it back. I begged and threatened her, but to no avail. For some reason, I lost interest in the beautiful key ring, and I let my daughter keep it. It seemed as if the desire for the gift was gone.

My daughter and I lived in the country in an apartment that used to be an office for a welding shop. We had two rabbits and the landlord agreed to let us have a pen next to the shop for the rabbits. There was a teen-aged boy who was the landlord's son who hung around the shop. My daughter was afraid of him because she said that he used drugs. My daughter wouldn't stay there alone even though we had a deadbolt lock on the door.

I was having my own Bible Study every night after I bought a Spirit Filled Life Study Bible. We were going to Wednesday night church and two services on Sundays. Somehow my daughter met a youth pastor from another church. One night this pastor and his wife came to visit my daughter and she felt so good about them. In my spirit, I felt there was something awry. They were a different denomination and I felt uneasy in what they believed in. She began to beg to go to their church and I told her that we should stay where we are for a while and not go from church to church. She was very angry with me on my decision.

Previously we had experienced an introduction to another denomination. About four months after I got saved, my youngest daughter also accepted the LORD. One evening she told me that a friend of hers was going to stop by. Within an instant, the doorbell rang, and here was her friend and her friend's mother. They wanted to speak to my daughter alone and I felt a check in my spirit. They were telling her about Jehovah and most of it didn't agree with what I read in my Bible.

After they left, my daughter told me that they were Jehovah Witnesses. The second time they came they were bolder and very emphatic about my daughter coming to their church. I asked them, "What do you believe in?" and they tried to avoid me. I approached them and they headed to the door.

I told my daughter, "Don't invite them here anymore, OK? They don't believe in our Bible, and their teachings are not from God but from man."

After speaking to her about the pastor and his wife from the other denomination, my daughter's anger escalated when I told her that we should not switch churches. I suggested to her that we should pray together and she shouted, "I don't EVER want to pray with you!" I told her that we are having some difficulties and prayer is the answer. Yet, she would not pray with me and I felt a huge distance between us.

There was so much oppression and darkness over that place in the country. We desperately wanted to get away from that place, especially after Snoopy, our rabbit, died. We had already given away our other rabbit. The reason for staying at that place was now gone since both of the rabbits were gone.

My daughter brought home a little gray kitten and we fell in love with it instantly. When the landlord saw the kitten, she got very angry and she made us give it back. Cats were not allowed at that place. I was very upset over her decision, and I was hoping that we could leave that place soon.

We were only four miles from town but my job required me to transfer to the capital city, which was 15 miles away from home. It was then that the landlord finally agreed that I could get out of my lease and we found an apartment in the city. The apartment that we found allowed cats, so we were able to get our kitten back. We felt very good about our move back into town.

On moving day I had everything moved out except for the big pieces of furniture, and I was waiting for my friend to come. This is the same friend who gave me the dream catcher. She was bringing her husband and her son to help lift my entertainment center and television.

All of a sudden I saw this black thing crawling around the baseboard in the living room. I had never seen a demon before, so I just stared. It was only about six inches high and I could see through it. It looked like a shadow of a small animal, something like a gremlin or a very small dog with pointy ears. It crawled alongside the wall and then it disappeared. I remember thinking: I wonder what that is. It seemed evil but I never experienced anything like that before. I had no fear but I couldn't seem to take my eyes off it. I remember thinking that it was good that we were leaving this place. Little did I know that we had something that belonged to the devil (the dream catcher) and this demon was welcome to come along to our new place, as we had something that belonged to him.

My daughter and I were very much involved in a Pentecostal church in the capitol city. I felt very close to God and I was part of the evangelism team. Every evening I had two Bibles on the kitchen table, along with a Bible reference book studying the Word.

My daughter came in and said to me in a sneering kind of voice, "So you think you are a Christian and that you are such a good person. Well, I know who you REALLY are!" The voice didn't sound anything like hers. It was cold and hard with no feeling.

I said to her, "I know that's not you talking but Satan himself. I don't believe anything you are saying. Get out, devil!"

She said, "OH!" in a disgusting way. She stomped off to her room and slammed the door.

My ex-husband filed for disability and he was approved during the time when my youngest daughter was 16 years old. She got a large sum of money, and I managed her money for her because she was still a minor.

This money was the beginning of a huge rift between my daughter and me. She wanted to take large amounts of money and spend it on whatever she wanted. I wanted her to save it to go college.

One of the first things that she wanted to buy was a car. We looked for about a week and found one, which turned out to be a lemon. The owner lied to us about the shape it was in, and it hardly ever started without being boosted first. We found a second car that was owned by a mechanic who worked for a Christian man, and I felt positive about this decision. Even so, there were also problems with this vehicle. It let her set many times after school in the parking lot.

I felt so sorry for my daughter. I was at work ten miles away, and it wasn't always easy to get away from the office without previous notice.

We had arguments every time my daughter wanted to buy clothes from the most expensive stores in Bismarck. Time after time, I relented, as it was her money. She had expensive taste, and I was sure that her money wouldn't last long. She was working for a department store in the jewelry department so she had other money to spend. Still, my daughter didn't want to live within her means.

Eventually she convinced me to take out all of the money out of the bank and spend it on a reliable vehicle, a little Geo Storm.

My daughter spent a lot of time in her room and she began to get more angry and vindictive towards me. We were still going to church and she was involved with the youth group. One day one of the kids in the youth group asked her if she was a newcomer, and she said, "No, I've been coming here for two years!"

That caused more anger, and she told me that she didn't want to go to church any more. I called the youth pastor and I asked him to call her. She couldn't understand why he would call her, so she asked him if I asked him to call. When he said, "Yes," that got her even angrier.

She began to date a boy in her Band class who wasn't a Christian. She told me she was in his bedroom and I told her that she shouldn't be there. She said that she knew how to handle herself, and that I didn't need to worry.

Within one month this young man was unfaithful to my daughter, and my daughter called him on the phone. She swore at him using all sorts of profanity, no holds barred.

I said to her, "Gee, why are you cursing like that? What's happened to you?" In so many words, she told me to mind my own business.

I have three daughters with the oldest one living in Minnesota at that time. My oldest daughter blamed me for the terrible childhood she had that was full of abuse from her father, and she was angry at me for accepting the LORD. We left their father when my oldest daughter was 13 years old.

We had many struggles after leaving their father. I was the only responsible parent. Many times I made poor choices, and we lived on Welfare for eight years. Some of that time I attended college and most of the time I never received any finances from their father. It was very difficult raising five children alone. I knew how my oldest daughter felt and that life seemed very unfair for her and her siblings. Still, my hands were tied until I could finish college and make a living on my own.

My oldest daughter constantly communicated with my youngest daughter, and they had a lot in common. They were both athletic and they went for 5-mile runs. Both of them were interested in nutrition and dieting. I didn't know it then, but my two daughters were conspiring against me. My oldest daughter called my youngest daughter when I was still at work, and they discussed that my youngest daughter should come live with her. This went on for months before I found out.

When my middle daughter got married in August that year, my youngest daughter told me that she wanted to live with her oldest sister.

I said, "Yes, you can after you finish high school." My youngest daughter said, "No, I want to go now." I said, "You can't go now." My daughter said, "Oh yes, I can! I have my own money, and I don't need you!"

The wedding was about six hours from home, and it was a long, silent trip back home. Not a word was said all of the way.

About two days later when my daughter came back from work at 11 pm, I told her that she has to finish high school at home with me. She was eating cereal out of a hard plastic measuring cup, and she threw it at me – cereal, milk and all. The milk dripped down my hair and from the tip of my nose. I remained calm and I didn't retaliate towards my daughter's undesirable behavior.

My daughter was screaming at me. "I hate you! I hate you! What kind of mother do you think you are? You're not my mother!"

I told her to keep her voice down because it was late with some other tenants trying to rest. She said, "I don't care! I'm not listening to you!"

I said, "If you don't stop it, I'm calling the cops." "Oh, now you want to be the authority!" she shouted.

I dialed the police station and they sent over two officers, one being female. I told them that she is not listening and they asked me what I wanted them to do. I just wanted them to talk to her, to calm her down.

My daughter sat down on the floor and took off her shoe. She threw her shoe across the room. The officer cuffed her and I asked, "What are you doing? Leave her alone. She'll be OK now."

They said, "No, she's violent and we're taking her in. You can call a family member to pick her up tonight. Do you have someone to call?" I said, "Yes, her uncle will come to pick her up."

Later in the week my daughter and I had to see a youth counsellor. I told him that I would allow her to live with her oldest sister. I didn't see the sense in arguing with my daughter for the next year until she graduated from high school in the following spring.

Within two days my daughter was gone and I felt so hurt and so much pain. The devil got a hold of her and I was at God's mercy. I needed healing and so did my daughters. I didn't know what to do but pray. I missed her so much. I cried almost every night. The people in church didn't understand, and I felt like they were blaming me for being a bad parent, and for being a single parent at that.

One night I felt so distraught and I asked God to help me. I put my hands over my eyes with tears running down my face. I was totally broken. God showed me my whole life in a moment of time. He sternly told me how he has always been there for me and He will lead me through this time also. From that time on, I leaned on the LORD for everything in my life. My daughter came to visit for a few minutes now and then, but nothing was resolved until ten years later.

I prayed for healing for our relationship and then I waited, as it says in the Word. "Wait upon the LORD."

One day in November 2006 I received a phone call from my daughter. She said, "Mom, can you ever forgive me?" When I heard those words, I held back the tears. It was then that she came back to the LORD, and now she is so in love with God.

Now we have a wonderful and open communication. Spiritually we are bonded. When one of us is in pain or is upset, the other one discerns the pain. We pray for one another regularly. We quickly caught up on the things that we missed during those ten years. I thank the LORD for my beautiful daughter and I love her so much. God gave my daughter back to me and with such a wonderful blessing. Words cannot describe the joy in my heart – the unspeakable joy!

Years before she threw away the dream catcher but the effects from it just about destroyed my daughter. The devil was out to kill her and he almost succeeded.

It never occurred to me at the time that such a small, harmless-looking gift could cause so much havoc in my daughter's and my life. In hindsight, our family breakup started right after I brought the dream catcher home. Today, after seeing many eye-witness experiences on how the devil can use anything spiritual belonging to him, I realize without a doubt that it was the devil that separated my daughter and me for so long."

SANCTIFYING AND CLEANSING

If you can sanctify and cleanse the unclean things you used for the devil and continue using this unclean thing, this unclean thing can't confess and repent like a human can, so why would you use this unclean thing in a holy place? When you do this, then it causes total confusion. Then explain why God desecrated the extinguished humans that sinned from the face of this earth; and why doesn't God just sanctify the earth and reuse it? In Revelation you read where John saw a new heaven and a new earth coming down out of heaven.

Don't believe anyone who says that Indian paraphernalia could be redeemed for the purpose of worshipping God. It's a lie. The enemy is only hiding himself only to attack later. All things that are originated by Indian beliefs have some spiritual attachment that comes with it. We have to separate ourselves totally from Indian religious beliefs.

I even had thoughts of going back to the sundance renaming it to "Sondance" that could be so easily done. I thought if I could just convince people that believe in the sundance. All the structure that's assembled together before the dancing represents the tabernacle of God, or I would have made up something else close to that my thought were bouncing off the walls trying to think up something to help God draw the lost. I would have been playing right into the hands of the devil himself. When you are young in Christ you think that you are doing God a favor in sitting up what you think could help God. I know for sure at that time that I was planning all these gimmicks to try and trick people into the kingdom of God. I limited God. I am talking about the Most High God, the Creator of heaven and earth including all men and everything else upon this earth and the heaven. Man, how foolish I was! I just could not see, my mind was not registering. Something must have gone completely wrong with my thinking. Like my dad (whom I call Dad who raised me) would say, "You need your head examined," because it's the same God that I mentioned that inspired the Holy Bible. He put this book together for us to grow spiritually in knowledge and in wisdom, everything that anybody needs.

> *"All Scripture is given by inspiration of God and is profitable for doctrine for reproof, for correction, for instruction in righteousness: That the man of God may be perfect, thoroughly furnished unto all good works."*[32]

> *"Then came Jesus scribes and Pharisees, which were of Jerusalem saying, Why do the disciples transgress the tradition of the elders? For they wash not their hands when they eat bread. But He answered and said unto them, Why do ye also transgress the commandment of God by your tradition? For God commanded, saying HONOR THY FATHER AND MOTHER and, HE THAT CURSETH FATHER OR MOTHER, LET HIM DIE THE DEATH, But ye say, whosoever shall say to his father or to his mother, It is a gift by whatsoever thou mightest be profited by me; And honor not his father or his mother, he shall be free. Thus have ye made the commandment of God of none effect by your tradition. Ye hypocrites,*

---

[32] 2 Timothy 3:16-17

well did E-sa-ias prophesy of you, saying THIS PEOPLE DRAWETH NIGH UNTO ME WITH THEIR MOUTH, AND HONOURETH ME WITH THEIR LIPS; BUT THEIR HEART IS FAR FROM ME.[20] *BUT IN VAIN THEY DO WORSHIP ME, TEACHING FOR DOCTRINES THE COMMANDMENTS OF MEN."*[33]

[33] Matthew 15:1-9

GIVE AWAY

I keep reiterating how subtle and crafty the enemy, the devil, Satan or the prince of the power of the air – whatever name you choose to call him. He has his hand into everything. It may look very small and harmless – whatever it is – but if it has any spiritual connection to it, he will use it, using subtlety and wisely, and so gradual that you don't even notice it move deeper and slowly deeper back into your daily life.

One of the many brothers in the Lord who lives a couple of hundred miles west of us once told a story while we were visiting them. They live in a trailer. The master bedroom is on one end of the trailer and three guest bedrooms on the other end. In between the bedrooms are the kitchen and the living room. Just before you enter into the kitchen on the master bedroom side there is a washer and dryer. The brother's wife, who also loves the Lord very much, was saying to my wife and I how she couldn't help but notice a very evil presence each time she walked by the washer and dryer. It was getting so that she half-ran across that small space between their bedroom and the kitchen.

She told her husband about it to see if he noticed anything. I guess to her surprise, he told her, "I thought I was just imagining it, but, yes, I did feel something weird there." He checked it out. He never noticed anything other than the usual things such as clothing, sheets and blankets. He couldn't understand why this was happening.

He said that one of his sons who stay there came home. He was going out on a camp job and he wanted to know if his mom washed the blankets.

His mom said, "No, I didn't do any washing yet." The son said, "Could you wash a blanket for me right away?" The mom said, "Where is your blanket?" I guess he said, "It is there by the washing machine."

She found a couple of blankets under a pile of clothes. She didn't recognize one of the blankets so she asked him, "Where did this blanket come from?" The son said, "It was given to me at the powwow during the giveaways."

The sister said, "You shouldn't have taken it. No wonder we were feeling evil coming from the laundry area. That blanket was there." The son responded, "Mom, it's only a blanket!'

The sister said, "It's only *just* a blanket? It belongs to the spirit world. This blanket was offered to spirits through prayers given to the spirits before they start giving them out. That is why the enemy had access to our house. Now, take it outside and burn it!"

So I guess the son got scared and he didn't want to burn it, lest he got a curse on him. His father escorted his son outside with the blanket and burned it, and afterward that evil presence was gone. This confirms the Scripture in Deuteronomy[34]:

> *"Neither shalt thou bring an abomination into thine house, lest thou be a cursed thing like it: but thou shalt utterly detest it, and thou shalt utterly abhor it; for it is a cursed thing."*

[34] Deuteronomy 7:26

RITUAL INDOORS

I am going to repeat a story from a dear brother in Christ who went home to be with Jesus. This brother lived in a town approximately forty miles west of our reservation. He is a First Nations man but he never got treaty status even though he proved to the Government that his grandfather was a status Indian from a reservation. The Government would not acknowledge this revelation, and he did not give up taunting the Government about his illegibility to be a status Indian right until the day he died.

In the meantime he learned all about the treaties made in Canada through thirty years of research. He also won a lot of court cases by using this information. Anyway, his relatives were all involved in the beliefs of our ancestors' spirituality. Some were what we used to call "powerful medicine men and medicine women". He grew up in all of this. He told me he was just a kid when he first witnessed a ritual done by one of his relatives. It was done inside a home made out of logs and rough lumber. This medicine man made a big feast dedicated to the grandfathers (ancestral spirits, spirit guides and mediums). In feasts like these the spirits always get the first servings.

They take a small portion from all of the food that is laid out. I mean, the living room floor is covered with what we call "Indian blankets" side by side lengthwise. On top of their blankets is this long tablecloth and it is full of every kind of food. It's like a pot luck dinner where all of the relatives pitch in and bring Indian delicacies – pails of special soups, a lot of canned fruits, wild berries, baked and fried bannock, cakes, cookies, pies, roasts of wild meat, potatoes and vegetables. The whole tablecloth is full. The peace pipe ceremony is done way before the feast starts. Also the offerings are already hung up. To confirm this story, I have also personally seen where a big bowl is full to the brim.

By the time the helpers are finished putting food in the bowl from a portion of all of the food put out on the tablecloth. Anyway he told me this big bowl of food is placed somewhere where no one will defile it. When all of the people and guests are done eating, they all pitch in and clean off the eating area, all except the Indian blankets. Then they take the bowl that was set aside and place it in the middle of those blankets. They darken the room by shutting out the daylight that shines through the windows with blankets, tarps, coats, etc., whatever helps to darken the room. After that is done, the medicine man prepares a small prayer to the grandfathers (spirit guides, ancestral spirits and medicine spirits) while holding a bowl in his hands which is smudged with sweet grass. After that is done the medicine man takes out his rattle (used for summoning spirits). Then the lights are shut off. It is pitch black inside. All you can hear is the medicine man chanting while shaking the rattle.

After the medicine man stops chanting, then some phenomenon happens. It's like an unknown force enters the room. You can even hear people moaning like they are trying hard to withhold fear or astonishment, although the medicine man warns not to fret if we hear strange sounds. It's only our grandfathers coming to the feast. Still, the presence of that force causes your heart to quicken.

It seemed that the rattle left the medicine man's hand, for the rattle started rattling up in the ceiling. Then the rattle starts moving around the room. The rattling of that rattle is so fast, and no human hands could rattle it like that. It starts circling the room. You can hear it go by above your head where you are sitting. The rattle spins around the room so quickly. The medicine man couldn't run around that room that fast without stumbling or stepping on someone. People are sitting on the floor along the wall when that rattle bumps into the wall or ceiling slightly. It causes sparks, like trying to light a lighter that doesn't have any fluid left. When that rattle went around the room four times, it stops.

Then when the medicine man got the rattle back, he shook it a couple of times and thanked the spirit. Then the presence of that force disappeared. After that the medicine man asked the helpers to open the lights, that "it is done", when they flick on the lights the bowl was sitting upside down in the same place it was when they shut off the lights. When the medicine man picked it up, the bowl was completely empty, and all of the food just vanished.

FINALLY ANOTHER MEDICINE MAN CONVERTED

I can never forget that time I received the Good News that one of the many medicine men that I knew so well got saved. I could hardly contain the joy I felt. I was shouting praises to God. I was overwhelmingly jubilant, thanking God for His loving, tender mercy. Finally I have someone that I can relate to. It sure made a difference for me – to have someone else that understood Indian religion to confirm my testimony.

I immediately started my wheels turning in search for my brand new brother. I actually met him during the many lodges, ceremonies and other activities and I knew where he was from, but I never knew exactly where he lived on that reservation. I started my search by phoning various brothers in Christ. I finally came across someone who had information on how to contact him.

It didn't take me long to contact the brother and right away he invited me to his home. When we finally met, he had on a big smile, and I never saw that kind of smile on his face before. We hugged each other, patted each other's backs, and I pushed him back at arm's length to take a good look, making sure it was really him. Oh my, what a happy reunion!

I said, "It's really you!" We laughed and hugged again. I said, "Welcome into the Kingdom of God! It feels good to see the work of God. It's a miracle!" From that day on, I never left him for long. I was always phoning, encouraging him and praying for him.

It seemed this brother started his walk four years ahead of his time. Most new converts start off with milk. He was entering a field unknown to him, so discretion was needed to be used in the process of step by step teaching of his new-found faith, which didn't happen for this brother. He had no Biblical teaching. All he had was the knowledge of our ancestral beliefs, yet he waged right into battle. He started way too fast with solid meat, then to milk, which probably contributed to his collapse later on.

He started organizing meetings by renting halls and churches, and we had a great time. He had special speakers come out now and then. We had some very powerful Spirit-packed meetings at times. I helped him every now and again whenever he needed special speakers. I would contact brothers that I knew who walked the narrow and the straight.

On occasion the enemy was also hard at work, disrupting his work. He tried discouragement during the preparation of upcoming events and fellowship meetings. At times he struggled to find finances and other distractions. In times like these I would edify the brother. I would tell him that this is to be expected when you are doing God's work. That is the devil trying to stop you, but don't let it slow you down. Keep on doing what is right for God. You are going to be rewarded for this by God in the end.

About three years later, it seemed that everything was going just fine for the brother. I started focusing more on my own ministry by going and venturing out wherever possible, a little more each time until things looked pretty stable for my Christian brother.

One time, possibly four years later, I spent a whole summer ministering in B.C. We had some awesome gospel meetings. What God did there is really worth mentioning at a one-week revival. The brother and his wife who set up these meetings started when he rented a hall for one full week. At the end of the week, we found out that the hall was rented for a wedding long before the brother rented it. No one had told us until Friday at the end of the revival that we couldn't use the hall on Saturday.

We couldn't just shut it down because the response to this revival grew in numbers. The hall was almost full to capacity and the people were getting so blessed by the moving of the Holy Spirit. We just couldn't suddenly quench the Spirit by discontinuing the flow. At the Friday night service the brother informed the congregation the news.

The summer days were hot and beautiful with no rain, and the evenings were just right for an open air meeting. He said, "We decided to hold the Saturday night meeting outside of my house." The brother had leased some land from a reservation where he had a trailer and about three or four houses on it. The houses were built side by side like a horseshoe shape, like a cul-de-sac. I remember that Saturday the brothers got together and started building a stage along the brother's house with scrap lumber. They even hooked up lights above the stage. They set up all the chairs in the opening of the cul-de-sac. That is where we held the Saturday night service and the place was packed. Every chair was taken. We had a rip-snortin', devil stompin' Holy Ghost meeting. When it was time for preaching, I was called to do the honors of preaching. In the middle of my preaching there were manifestations of evil spirits that started moving.

There were mostly women that had these evil spirits manifesting. They were screaming, yelling, and shouting words like, "No! No! Leave me alone!" They were thrashing around. One woman was using a cane since she could barely walk. She threw the cane way up high and away from everyone there and started jumping around.

Here is the part that I really want to mention. Just as I was through praying for the people approximately five police cars pulled in. Somebody had reported a drunken riot happening. The police didn't know what was going on. There was no sign of booze or anyone drunk, even after we explained that we were having church. There were a lot of Indians living there because it was on a reservation right along a busy highway close to a small city. What else could happen but an eye-gouging, drug out fisticuffs on an Indian reservation during a drinking party? With all of the commotion and ruckus we were making, it must have sounded like a Saturday night drunken brawl. Eventually we convinced the police. Maybe they were relieved, too. They maybe assumed the worse possible case scenario, and they were geared up for it. But praise the Lord, it was a party, a Holy Ghost Party!

At the end of that particular summer, I finally got back home when snow was already on the ground. I am blessed to have my youngest son to stay home to watch over my home whenever we are on the road.

I got things organized at home before I decided to phone my brother. He had been on my mind for a while before I thought of coming back to Alberta, my home province in Canada. When I finally contacted him, I felt this grief in my spirit. Before he even started talking and when he knew who was calling, his response wasn't like the other times. He didn't greet me like he used to, the joy was gone. He spoke like he couldn't care less who I was. Right away I knew something was wrong. He wasn't the happy person that I knew before I left. He's a brother that I kid around with a lot, and we had happy times together.

I said, "What's wrong? What's going on?" He said, "Well, maybe it will be better if you come down and see for yourself. I have some visitors right now and I can't stay on the line too long to explain. Do you think maybe you can come down tomorrow early, like before noon?" I said, "Yes. I'll make sure that I do. I'll be there." He said, "Okay. I'll be seeing you tomorrow."

He didn't even say "brother" or anything to indicate I was a friend. Then I said, "All right, brother, I'll see you then." And we hung up. I had an uneasy feeling and I knew in my spirit that something was troubling him. He must have fallen into the hands of the enemy, and if he had, it could be any of several factors to blame. I wouldn't know that for sure until I hear all of the facts, so I'll just have to wait. It couldn't be done from the unsaved, like me, when I first renounced Indian religion.

I encountered many attacks from medicine men and medicine women trying to throw fear into what I had done. They tried in vain to scare me back – back to the Indian religion with no results. He had gone through the same attacks. I fell (as it is mentioned in my first book) but it wasn't a medicine man or a medicine woman that caused me to fall. The devil used a Bible thumping, hell stomping, fire a brimstone preacher. Even during the darkest times in my backsliding state, I never once considered the Indian religion as a power to fall back into.

I remember that it was tried on him many times before I left. He'd just smile and say, "The lies of the enemy." He knew the world system never had the answer then, but God knows what all else came after I left. Even though religion is still the lies of the enemy, it is more subtle because Scriptures can be used to beguile the newly saved or even one that's lukewarm, that had put the Bible aside to use whenever he felt like it – I mean, one that isn't grounded in the Word.

Remember the enemy, the devil can also quote Scripture. The devil quoted a Scripture to Jesus when he was tempting Him in:

> *"For it is written, 'He shall give His angels charge over Thee, to keep Thee, 11and in their hands they shall bear Thee up, lest at any time Thou dash Thy foot against a stone.' "*[10]

These same Scriptures can be found in:

> *"And even his ministers can preach righteousness."* [11]

I made sure that I got up bright and early for the visit. I was sort of excited in anticipation of what I felt happened. He was also an early riser, so I left right after a small breakfast. I got there around 8 a.m. and, sure enough, he was all set to meet the day.

I was happy to see him again, although he never showed any sign that he did. He just told me to come in, not like before. He'd be opening the door for me or if it was summer, he'd be outside to greet me. Anyway he offered me coffee and we sat down at the dinner table and started talking. I told him all about my time of ministering in B.C., and he started telling me about what took place in his life since the last time we were together.

For a while good things were happening until one day his wife got mixed up with this New Age group, and because of it she got lured into believing the doctrine she heard. That really turned her completely in the wrong direction. It was a teaching she heard from the group that it was all right to mix her old Indian religious beliefs with Christianity. They somehow convinced her and she decided to try it out and she became a medium in the process of going back to her old ways. I guess there were many strange things occurring spiritually, which put the final confirmation to what the New Age group taught her to believe. Gradually my brother got sucked into trying it out also.

If this sounds familiar, it's because this same thing happened with Adam and Eve:

> *"And when the woman saw that the tree was good for food, and that it was pleasant to the eyes, and a tree to be desired to make one wise, she took of the fruit thereof, and did eat. And*

> *gave also unto her husband with her; and he did eat."*[35]

He was snared right back in doing what God had brought him out from. What really cinched it were the supernatural occurrences that immediately followed.

He told me a short story that can be explained if a person is grounded in the Word. To him it was unexplainable, a mystery which caused him to be in awe.

He told me that he had gone back to the sweat lodge. He said this bright light entered his sweat lodge and he kept his eyes closed because the light was so bright, and a terrifying fear came upon him that he almost lost his consciousness. That light stayed for approximately 15 to 20 minutes before it left and he said he didn't know what that light was. He turned to his wife, the medium, for answers and the spirits spoke through her and told him that it was the Angel of God whom he interpreted as Jesus Christ Himself.

The brother was past the point of reasoning when this happened. He had already formed a callous heart. His ears were plugged up with wax and he had a very stiff neck. He never even for a moment stopped to think this out. It could mean life or death, yet instead of seeking God for an answer, he did the unthinkable by turning to a medium (his wife) for answers. Just what kind of an answer would anybody in his right mind expect from a medium? A medium is not of God in the first place. I am sure the Lord was not agreeing on what the brother was doing. When this bright light appeared, I would have taken it as a stern warning that I was committing high treason, that I was in the wrong place doing the wrong thing. All because when the spirit of God is present, you feel an overwhelming peace and an unspeakable overflowing joy, not a terrifying fear like the brother described.

---

[35] Genesis 3:6

Another thing that bound his mind was the unquestionably fact that the spirits confirmed that Jesus Christ had entered his lodge. You see, he took this as a sign that he made the right decision. He tried telling me because of this, that these spirits were holy spirits that spoke through his wife.

I said, "Listen, brother, even the devils know God and they tremble."

> *"The devils also believe and tremble."*[36]

"Don't you remember reading in the Word where the unclean spirits identify Jesus Christ as the Son of the Most High God?"

They said,

> *"When he saw Jesus, he cried out and fell down before Him, and with a loud voice said, 'What have I to do with Thee, Jesus, Thou Son of God Most High? I beseech Thee, torment me not.'* "[37]

But I could tell in the way he smiled (because I saw this same smile so many times before) that he wasn't at all going to consider what I was trying to expound. He used this same smile when he was skeptical in what I just told him. I know when this brother smiles that way that he is actually saying, 'I know where this is leading to. Don't try and con me. I know what I'm doing.'

It was then that I knew that he turned away from God. This man was wounded deeply and hurt by his own, and he was never coming back. I could see that I was too late.

He told me a story about angels guarding his driveway. He said, "I could see them from the house. They were like northern lights in a form of human bodies, some standing

---

[36] James 2:19

[37] Luke 8:28

and some walking back and forward at the gate of my driveway."

By then I was so hurt of what was happening to my dear brother. I was all choked up, watching him being deceived. I was far away in my own thoughts in a pain that I have never felt before for a brother. I could hardly believe that this was happening.

Another big factor in his turning his back on Jesus was the doctrine's denominations he was bombarded with. He was young in the Lord and mighty good things were happening in his life.

When Christian brothers and sisters in the Lord, preachers, evangelists and pastors heard of this mighty revival happening at this brother's place during Bible Studies or sometimes they held gospel meetings at his home, they all flocked to his place. I was also there every time because the brother and I had a good communication going since we both came out of Indian religion.

Man, I tell you, it was more like an arguing place. He was just a babe in Christ and all of a sudden he was involved in a different level of spiritual doctrine. Every kind of denomination from different churches came to express their knowledge of the interpretation of Bible passages. I remember at times there were heated arguments to prove a point from the Word of God.

I clearly recall one small group who attended those Bible Studies. They were in deliverance. They told the brother that his wife needed deliverance, especially this one man who proclaimed he had experience in deliverance. He said that he was going to show us how it was done.

I have never seen deliverance done this way since that time. The house was packed out with Christians. We were all seated in chairs in a circle. This brother brought the brother's wife in the middle of this circle, grabbed the sister and threw her to the floor. We all watched in anticipation, probably hoping to witness a manifestation of unclean spirits. This was totally out of the ordinary.

The sister was caught completely by surprise, too. She must have been like the rest of us. We didn't know what was happening, and she fought back like her life was depending on it.

That White brother got the surprise of his life, too. This sister was no weakling. No sooner landing on the floor she flipped the White brother just as fast and he was underneath her from that time on. Back and forward they took turns landing underneath. Once in a while you could hear the brother begging for help, but no one came to his aid.

Looking back on this scenario brings a smile to my face. In retrospect, it was ridiculously hilarious. It was a scene taken out of a comedy show because nothing happened – just a wrestling match.

The sister finally called her husband to get that man off her. I think the brother was more than happy to do this. He grabbed that White brother, and just threw him off his wife and the brother shouted at the White brother, "That's enough! Now get the *!## out of my house. Don't you ever show your face here again!" And he escorted him out by the cuff of his neck.

I don't know from what teaching he got this from, but it was without a doubt false. It sure didn't line up with the Word. Does it say in the Bible that Jesus had a wrestling match with some human? No, He just commanded the unclean spirits to come out.

Anyway it was these kinds of instances that helped drive the brother back into the world. I am sure you know what I am talking about. We all were babes in Christ at one time – what we heard and learned. At the very beginning some of what we heard was found to be wrong after we matured in the Word of God.

This brother was bombarded with every kind of teaching to a point that he just lost it and gave up. It's like anything else, when you had a bad experience with something, you just don't like to go back to it. You find something else to your liking. All the people that came to the brother's home probably thought they were helping him. Don't get me wrong. Some were true Christians mixed in with whoever attended those gatherings, but it did more damage to the brand new brother.

These unsturdy conflicts pertaining the Bible Scripture from Christians and supposedly Christians led to the demise which resulted in the brother's fall. I know even scholars and theologians have their disagreements showing different points of view on Biblical interpretation. Such was the case when I took it upon myself to search out when the rapture was really going to take place – before the seven-year or halfway through the seven-year or after the seven-year tribulation. I bought books written by scholars and theologians and read through all of them. They all believed there was going to be a rapture. They also all had different times using the same Scriptures. This confused me but it didn't cause a reason to fall. I hung on to my salvation.

So when his wife decided to try out and practice the old ways again, it didn't take much to lure my brother back to something he was brought up in – something that he understood, where no one could tell him what to do. This caused him to abandon Christianity. He went back to what he knew best and he never looked back. We lost him to the devil, which kind of reminds me of the Scripture.

> *"Woe unto you, scribes and Pharisees, hypocrites! For ye compass sea and land to make one proselyte, and when he is made, you make his twofold more the child of hell than yourselves."*[38]

---

[38] Matthew 23:15

You see, I am writing this in deep sadness and sorrow, for the whole family of this one-time brother – three sons, one daughter, his wife and himself are all dead. This brother wasn't very much older than I, probably six or seven years older. I know that they would all be alive today and doing well. That's what caused the sorrow for them.

The One-time Happy Praising Jesus Family is gone from the face of the earth. All died in rebellion. I heard he was back playing music in dance halls, back in bingo halls, casinos and horse races with his wife. Their kids were all into drugs and died in it, his wife died of diabetes and he died of a massive heart attack, which confirms this:

> *"But he that received the seed into stony places, the same is he that heareth the word, and anon with joy receiveth it; 21yet hath he not root in himself but dureth for a while: for when tribulation or persecution ariseth because of the word, by and by he is offended)"* [39] [20]

and also

> *"He also that received seed among the thorns is he that heareth the word: and the care of this world and the deceitfulness of riches choke the word and he becometh unfruitful. "*[40]

What really came in handy for the brother was the fact he was a musician before he met the Lord. Because of this, he had a lot of music equipment with him, not like me. When I set up gospel meetings, I had to find a gospel band for backup music and worship. This brother could do part of the gospel service that he set up. Sometimes you could hear this brother sing a gospel song on a local radio station here in Edmonton, Alberta, Canada. He was doing well for

[39] Matthew 13:20-21
[40] Matthew 13:22

the Lord. He had fire in his bones, it seemed like, at the time when God was blessing, until the enemy came and infiltrated himself back into his life...

> *To kill, steal and destroy the whole family.*[41]

This confirms the Scripture:

> *"Afterward Jesus findeth him in the temple, and said unto him, Behold, thou art made whole: sin no more, lest a worse thing come unto thee."*[42]

[41] John 10:10
[42] John 5:14

SPECIAL SISTER IN CHRIST

I have a sweet, loving sister in Christ who stood by me steadfast to the ministry that God has given me. She supported the ministry without wavering nigh unto twenty five years now. Not only financially, but through edification, exhortation, prayer and rebukes when it was needed, she stood strong through it all. She helped so much, especially during the time my first wife went home to be with Jesus. She did her best to comfort me through this heartbreak, sorrow and pain. She cried along with me. She guided me through near mishaps with her wisdom and knowledge. She was never afraid to speak her mind to me, and today I am very happy that I listened to her. She is a very special sister to me. Sometimes I dread the day when she goes home to be with Jesus.

We both came through a lot of trials, tribulations and persecution during that time. Like me, her parents were deeply rooted in the religion of our ancestral beliefs, traditions and spirituality. Although she herself became a born again believer early in her life and she was never involved in her parents' beliefs, her parents continued their involvement in the practices of their ancestral beliefs of the Indian spirituality in the religion of their forefathers. Her father was well known as a very powerful spiritual leader, highly regarded individual, well respected in all aspects as far as Native spirituality goes in Indian country. He sat among our political leaders in big gatherings as their elder, and he was also known to be a clairvoyant.

Prayer and the peace pipe ceremony were compulsory to begin these conferences done by the big Indian institutions. These conferences deal solely on providing the necessary training to sober individuals who at one time were alcoholics and drug addicts themselves. Not only was he chosen to do the prayer and the peace pipe ceremony, but he also was selected to speak and teach.

I recall seeing him when I was in my first years of sobriety. I had a personal vendetta against alcohol (just as I have today against the lies of the devil), because it took so many of my loved one's lives. I got so involved in the war against alcoholism and drug addiction. I had given my life to battle against this enemy of alcohol and drugs. It was also at the height of my involvement in the Indian religion, and I practiced it to the uttermost. It was during this time of my life that I went to big conferences.

The foundation of the substance abuse programs was based on Indian spirituality, which is the tradition and culture. This is where he sat as the head medicine man as an elder chosen by the alcoholism program directors. This training was so much needed in Indian country throughout all of Canada.

Because of this upbringing she understands very well what we are up against in our Christian walk. Because of this we are in one accord when it comes to understanding the spiritual warfare. When a strange occurrence happens, otherwise unexplainable to a person without spiritual knowledge, she would disclose such stories to me. She used to tell me that she thought that she could have both worlds when she first started her Christian walk after she became born again.

As a traditional dancer, she said she loved powwows before she came to Christ. So when the change took place from the spirit of the world to God's Holy Spirit, she felt like dancing with more enthusiasm and agility than ever. She thought that was what she was supposed to do, so she continued without questioning if that was okay to do this. She said she used to be anxious and excited when she heard of a powwow coming up.

She traveled to faraway places to dance in these powwow circuits throughout the years, until one day the Lord finally got her attention. She was hit by a curse. She was taking part in a powwow in the neighboring province of Saskatchewan when this happened.

Wait, I got to backtrack a little bit. She told me of another experience she had during dancing right in the arena. This man came up behind her and nudged with a whistle stick. When she turned her head to look, she found herself staring into the eyes of a man who became her second husband. Her first husband died years before. She said she had no intentions of ever marrying again. She knows today that she was set up by this man long before he made this effort to nudge her. It was mind control witchcraft because she just fell head over heels in love. That nudge just sent love shivers all through her body especially the mind, and secondly that curse almost destroyed her.

She said she was all dressed up in her regalia anxiously walking toward the arbor when suddenly she felt this twinge under her feet and the next step she took her leg gave way and she just collapsed. Her legs lost their power, it was like her strength from her legs were drawn away or drained. Instantly her legs ballooned like they were going to explode. With it came this excruciating extremely agonizing pain that almost stopped her heart. The throbbing was so intense that she was moaning with each breath she took. Her husband had to carry her back to their tent. When they knew there was no help for her, once again her husband carried her to their vehicle and left the powwow and started for back home. All the way back she said she was crying out in pain.

It wasn't until they were almost home that whatever it was that had her in bondage lifted just as quickly as it happened. She said that's when she finally turned to the Lord for her answers. She says that it was quite a valuable lesson she learned that day. She had left a door open when she continued powwow dancing.

She didn't leave the old way behind like the Scripture says, "You have become a new creature. Behold, old things must pass away, behold, all things must become new." She left herself vulnerable for this curse to happen. Once she found out the dangers in participating in secular activities, she said she abandoned all traditional and competition powwow dancing and put away her regalia and burned it up. She never ever again had that desire of dancing. It was completely taken away.

Another time she told me this story. "It was like a dream," she said, "but it was so real. I am sure it actually happened." Like the apostle Paul in 2 Corinthians 12:3 "And I knew such a man (whether in the body, or out of the body, I cannot tell: God knoweth)".

It was so clear and precise in what she saw that night. Everything she saw was so defined, a clear description from above, even though it was during the night. "I saw roads, lakes, towns, rivers and small streams just as clear as day. This evil force, a spirit of some sort, came into my room. I was already in bed, waiting to fall asleep when it took me right out of my house through the roof and headed straight west toward the mountains." Before she can even react they reached what seemed like its destination.

High above where this evil force tried pulling her down into this dark hole was the center of the Indian settlement. She believes medicine men were doing a ritual and they were about to pull her down into a lodge prepared especially for this purpose. This was possibly enticed by someone who knew her. She knows medicine men or medicine women don't do these rituals at random. It's caused from sheer vengeance or they were hired by someone. Only God knows because somehow this force just couldn't pull her down.

They had her there, above that lodge but they didn't have the spiritual power to defeat her protection. She didn't know just exactly how long they tried. Eventually, she saw the structure of that lodge flatten and collapse to ruins, leveled to the ground. Only then this force released her. She found herself back in her house.

She used to tell me she had a daughter living in that settlement that she prayed for many years, praying that she would leave that place and move out. She claimed that her daughter was taken under a spell by the man her daughter lived with on that settlement. No human being in her right mind would suffer under such extreme physical abuse daily, year after year and still remain loyal to her spouse. She used to say it was mind control bondage through witchcraft and sorcery. There is no other answer.

She figures her prayers were finally been slowly answered and her supposedly son-in-law detected something was amiss, probably a change he noticed in the actions of his tormented common-law wife that made him sought after an answer which made him turn to the medicine men, which transpired into this ordeal to take place.

I am sure if I were that medicine man that tried bringing my sister in Christ into the lodge I have prepared and failed, I would have blamed myself. As medicine men we would never give the benefit of the doubt to the other party. We would never admit defeat. Like I said, if I were that medicine man or maybe a medicine woman for all I know, but it's still dealing with the spirit world no matter which sex tried – male or female – so I would probably blame my frame of mind, like did my mind stray on something else. Was I distracted during the preparation of this ritual? Was I clean?

The rule is most times you have to abstain from having sex with your spouse at least a month before doing a ritual after her last menstruation to make sure you are not defiled, and a lot of times it may be much longer. This is compulsory but that depends on what kind of ritual you are doing.

Or maybe the color of prints. Did I get the colors required, etc. You blame these sorts of things. Like I've been saying the grandfathers (the spirits) are very strict in matters pertaining to what is prepared for them. Because this has been in our families for generations, we are supposed to know precisely what we are supposed to do. When something fails, this is what you look for. Everything comes into play.

It's not only what I mentioned here – there are many other things I hadn't disclosed that could be faulted. You never say her power was much more powerful than mine. I know God always has a purpose in matters such as this. These elders know that our sister is a Christian. They know now how powerful is the power that protects the Christians.

PERFECT LOVE CASTS OUT FEAR

Like I said, I have one sister in my family, and she's in her 70's now. Every now and then she phones me. Although she lived just next door where my mother used to live, it seemed we had no time to visit each other. Once in a while we'd both be outside and all we did was wave. I know for a fact she would be visiting me, but she was terribly afraid of dogs. We have three dogs – two outside and one little dog inside. While she was on the phone, she started telling me this story.

She said she saw a black dog standing on the road while she was going somewhere on foot. The dog was approximately seventy-five yards in the direction she was going. "I kept my eye on this dog. It glanced my way once and disappeared. It walked off the road into the ditch, into some tall grass."

"I kept going and when I got to where I last saw the dog, it was lying in the ditch. It suddenly jumped up to its feet as if someone kicked it, and it started looking my way. It looked uneasy with uncertainty, but it was really staring. It seemed like it wasn't looking at me but at something or someone else besides me. It saw something other than me, but yet I was all alone. It seemed it couldn't quite make out what that thing was. The dog had a puzzled look. It also looked like it was ready to attack whatever it was this dog saw."

"I thought maybe this dog might decide to attack me instead, so I quickened my steps to get past him as fast as I can. If it decides to attack me, I had nothing with me to beat him off with. This dog definitely saw something."

"At another time I was walking around the central part of the community. A cluster of houses and trailers, the administration office and the health center, etc., are all located in this area. Here you can find plenty of dogs roaming all over. I met this little dog coming down this walking trail and there were people going to and fro to these offices all day long. This dog was sniffing the ground paying no mind to the people walking by him until it got to me."

"All of a sudden it jumped to the side of the walking trail and stared. It wasn't staring into my eyes like most dogs do. It was staring at the mid-section of my body. It proceeded to walk very gently and carefully around me like it was preparing to strike at any moment. All the while it was growling. She said she was just telling the dog, "Get away from me! Get away, you evil dog! Go on! Git!"

"The dog acted like it never heard a word. All it was doing was focusing on what it was that it saw around me. After I was a ways past him, I looked back. The dog was still looking my way."

She said this is why she gets afraid of dogs, not knowing what they just might decide to do.

While she was on the phone talking to me, she heard our Poodle/Chihuahua raising a ruckus. She said, "You mean to tell me you got a dog inside too? No wonder I don't go there. If they don't get me outside, they are surely gonna get me inside!" (meaning the dogs)

I started to laugh at her comment and I heard her laugh on the other end, too. I knew she was laughing at me, because she could read my thoughts. She knew I was laughing at her foolish thinking. While we were on the subject of dogs, I started telling a story about a brother who pastors a big church in Gallup, New Mexico. I guess he goes out ministering around the local communities to the Indian people. He said that one night while traveling to one of the places, he almost rear-ended this great big dog, trotting down the middle of the highway. This was a huge black dog, as big as a Saint Bernard or probably bigger.

He said, "When I got there, I told this brother about this dog that I narrowly missed. This was the biggest dog I ever saw in my life." The brother stopped what he was doing and looked at me and said, "Was this dog's hind end swaying as it was trotting?" I said, "Yeah, it was. How do you know?"

"Because this isn't just a dog. It's someone who shapeshifted into a dog. That's how they run when a human shapeshifts."

I guess the brother was questioning him in amazement on how they do this, and he answered and went into some detail where a human is so possessed that he eats the remains of a dead relative before he or she can accomplish this belief brought down by their ancestors.

As I know without a doubt that the enemy (the devil) is obligated to oblige to these beliefs to keep them in the dark and in bondage away from the truth (God's Word). Those that are involved in this practice are positively convinced that this ancestral way passed down from generations of practice is the chosen path. Believe me, I was there.

When I mentioned to her about the medicine man who shapeshifted in my first book, I heard my sister say, "That man was with another medicine man at one time, and they did a spiritual ceremony for their grandfathers (ancestral spirits) in one of the gathering places in our family's hunting areas."

"They had a big feast first before a ritual dance. These two men were given soup made in water pails, and these pails were full." She continued to say, "These two men stuck their hands elbow deep into the soup pail proceeding to break up chunks of meat into tiny pieces."

When they were done, they grabbed the pail (they each had a pail) with both hands on each side of the pail, lifted it to their mouths and started to drink the soup until it was completely empty without stopping. When they set their pails down, they pretended to kick one another just like horses do, and they both made a sound like a horse squealing when they are going to kick each other.

When the dance started they gave a drum to one of these medicine men. Then he got his helpers to sit down in a circle with him and he started his song. No sooner had he started that we heard this horse neigh, which happened to be this medicine man's horse. These people that were outside this huge teepee where the ritual was done saw this horse in full gallop bucking and kicking and squealing toward the tent and sharply skidded to a stop right against the tent next to where his owner was singing and stood there. When the song was done, it was the other medicine man's turn to sing, and the exact same thing happened. His horse also came and stopped next to the first horse. These two horses stood there all through the ritual until it was done. Many of the Indian people grew up seeing these false signs and wonders, sight and sounds to a point it don't phase them any more – it doesn't surprise us at all. We just know it is supposed to happen this way because we've been taught since childhood. We never questioned how these manifestations came about until, of course, a person finds the real power Jesus Christ. Then as years follow, these mysteries start unraveling until it is totally revealed. The culprit? The devil himself.

She also told me a sad story about this real smart dog that she remembers they had as a child. My father, my oldest brother and my uncle (my father's youngest brother) were out beaver trapping in early spring. They brought this dog along.

She was telling me this dog was an amazing dog. It did a lot of things to help. It would swim and retrieve ducks that were shot on a lake or a pond, and also retrieve beavers that were shot dead in the rivers or ponds. It would tree partridge and lynx, it was a sleigh dog, and at last a pack dog. It also protected us, she said. Because of this usefulness they brought this dog along. She said there was one problem with this dog. If you tied him up with a rope, it would gnaw on the rope until he'd chewed it off and release itself.

Sometimes it would pull on the knot and untie himself. You could never keep it tied up for long. On their way back after approximately three weeks on my dad's trapline they came to the Athabasca River. Normally this river is very dangerous during early spring when the ice just broke up. It is high and very fast. I recall sitting on a hill in view of this raging river as a young man, watching the big chunks of ice bobbing and colliding with each other with great big crashing sounds as they hit one another. It was fascinating and frightening to watch, huge trees and stumps, all kinds of debris just flying down that river. It is impossible to even think of crossing this river in early spring. You could also hear this river a quarter of a mile before you came to it during this time of the season.

In late spring you wouldn't believe it's the same river. It slows right down and it is as tame as can be. You can see sandbars and small rock islands here and there. There are also fairly big-sized islands all the way down this big river.

My dad, his youngest brother and my oldest brother made themselves a big raft out of dry trees they found along the river. They decided to float down the river until such time they got near a road. At that time they were looking for a spot to anchor their raft when they came upon an island in the river where they decided to stop.

It was approximately around noon. They thought it would be a good place to have lunch, so they anchored their raft tied it up and unloaded their packs that had their provisions. They also unloaded their guns, axes to cut firewood and such that came along, like making tea. Sometime during the preparation my oldest brother went to the raft to pick up something. He got there in time to see their raft disappearing around the bend of the river with the dog still tied to the raft.

My sister said to me, “That’s how it always was. We could never have a dog that lived out their lives with our family. Somehow we were just unlucky with dogs.” To even imagine what took place with this dog -- untying the rope that held the raft instead of himself. What happened afterward only God knows. The raft might have stayed on the river for miles and the dog got himself loose or the raft might have jammed up and the dog probably untied himself and got to safety. The chances were great – at least a 95% chance -- that the dog got away. It was a big raft and it couldn’t have capsized. The dog never came home and all of the pelts were lost to the river.

Another story is about a dog also that my sister mentioned that Mom told. This one had to do with our parents’ spirituality. The story goes back to our great grandmother. This story took place during midwinter. They were out on their hunting grounds trapping. They had their base camp set up along a small lake in a big ti-pi. It was all insulated with extra thick blankets on the inside and banked up with snow on the outside. At the time the men and their wives went further north to spend a week or two depending on how good trapping was at the place they went. They left my great grandmother and the children, for they had plenty of food. A few days had gone by when their bitch dog started howling. This howling carried on for several days, and my great grandmother found it very strange for this dog to do that. While she was in bed listening to this dog one night, this strange feeling came over her that sent shivers through her body. She got up and told her grandchildren, “There is something wrong about this dog. I feel it’s trying to communicate with us. I’ll have to try something.”

Right away she put some food together, took out her medicine bundle and prepared a peace pipe ceremony. After the ceremony was done, she brought out the food for the dog. While she was feeding the dog, she was talking to the dog.

"Whatever it is that is causing you to act this way, I want you to share it tonight. I will make a pledge to put up offerings for this purpose when we finish trapping and sell the furs."

With that said, she went back inside and put away her medicine bundle and went to bed. That night in a dream the dog spoke to her. It said, "I have been crying out for my little ones. (Apparently this dog had some pups). They are going to be slaughtered including you and your grandchildren. A war party of your most feared enemy is headed this way, and they are not far off as of right now, about a day after tomorrow they are going to hit this lake and they are going to find us."

This happened sometime in the 1800's when there was still a lot of hostility among the different Indian tribes. Right here, right now, on the Reservation if you get into a physical confrontation, it's likely you will start a family war. This is how volatile our environment of this Reservation is. Again, this is the code of ethics. It's like this one brother told me while I was ministering in New Mexico, "You see that vast empty land out there? Well, it looks like nobody owns it because there is nothing but open space on it. But just try building something on it."

I mention this passage of Scripture many times over.

> *"Be not deceived: God is not mocked, for whatsoever a man soweth that shall he also reap."*[43]

This dislike and vengeance to prove superiority to show dominance among certain tribes has been in the bloodline for generations. This tribe of warriors in this story according

[43] Galatians 6:7

to tribal history was fierce, always looking for weaker tribes to destroy, looking for blood although they were not as powerful as being fierce, but they were persistent in looking for trouble. According to the history of this tribe, they were from the east that settled in northern border of what is now the United States, probably around Montana.

Anyway my great grandmother was trapped with her own grandchildren in the middle of the winter. If she was by herself, she probably might have eluded her enemies, but with innocent little children, it left her with no options at all. The only alternative was to consult with the dog.

She asked, "What are the chances of surviving?" The answer was, "None." "But I'd like to try something. It may work. Tomorrow when it gets toward evening I want you to take all of your bedding, bring it to the lake and make your bed among those cattails and bring my little ones along. Make sure you hide all of your provisions."

She did everything as instructed. That night around midnight a light breeze started. The cattails began to rustle and gradually it started to snow. Toward morning the wind became a north wind and started really blowing. There was a big blizzard and the snow started really coming down. This blizzard created huge piles of snow drifts which completely covered them. This snow and blizzard did not stop until there was no sign of human life. Then there was only silence.

Our great grandmother really expounded to the children that no matter what they hear happening, don't make a sound. So sometimes during the later afternoon they started hearing people talking and walking on top of the snow drift. Although my great grandmother tried her best to make it look like they had abandoned this place long ago, but still their enemy was acting on a notion.

Because the enemy didn't want to leave until all possibilities were tried to prove that there were no people there, they got themselves long dry rails from young trees and started poking holes through the snow drift all along the area of the lake where the ti-pi was. According to our great grandmother, they also hit their target several times. When the enemy was satisfied there was no one around, they finally left. Our great grandmother waited until nightfall when she was sure that the enemy was gone before they came out of hiding.

This is only one story of many encounters with this same tribe. There are also other stories my mother told me about how some of her relatives interpret animal sounds, e.g., a wolf howling or a coyote making weird sounds, a bear, etc. Sometimes it's a warning of some sort or about a family tragedy, like news told to them ahead of time.

NECROMANCY

You see, my sister is positively sure that a curse was spoken on her life, because she suffered unexplainable pain of all sorts throughout all of her life. She is quite sure this curse started when she was just a young teenager, at the very early age of thirteen when she was already with a husband. She always said she was never given a chance in life to meet and select a man she would marry. She felt cheated in that area of her life because in those days a man was chosen for you by your parents.

Anyway, she told me that all her in-laws were working in a lumber camp that winter, just west of a little oil town called Cynthia, close to the Rocky Mountains. They used to call this camp "Prop's Camp". It was situated along the Pembina River. The land and forest was just beautiful and it was virgin timber. There were only winter roads, unlike today where the oil roads are side by side criss-crossing every which way. Almost all of those beautiful hills are clear cut by huge lumber industries. It's hard to describe the terrible mess. It is completely beyond repair. Anyway, a lot of money was made by the Indians that winter.

Another thing that was done during that winter was some of the older men and women got together and started some card game tournaments just for leisure activities. They played cribbage, trump, 50 Points, bridge, etc. Then there were also hand games and for those that enjoyed gambling, they had poker games. A few times they had a round dance. They had feasts when someone shot game and you can't leave out booze parties, although the Treaty Indians were not allowed in the hotels and bars in those days. (The bars weren't open for Treaty Indians until 1966 in Canada.) The time I am talking about was around 1947 to 1948. The Indians had to rely on the White Man for their booze. The truckers that hauled the lumber would take their orders and money. This is how they got booze into the camp.

Then one day one of the men from our group started having problems with his legs. It seemed like all of his strength in both legs went weak. He couldn't work, and somehow they managed to send a message to a medicine man from back home to come. It wasn't long when this medicine man arrived in camp to doctor this man, although this medicine man was actually from another reservation just south of ours. The majority of the people there spoke the Nakota Sioux language. It happened this medicine man spoke both languages – Cree and Nakota Sioux. During the time he was doctoring this one person, he also started doctoring other people. It wasn't long before he started doing rituals.

This is where a *ti-pi* is put together, particularly for summoning spirits. I know many in Indian country heard this saying, "a tying is going to be done". That means that a medicine man is going to be tied with rawhide ropes, bound hand and foot where the knots are so tight that no human could undo these knots, not unless they are cut off. Then the helpers carry this medicine man and throw him inside this *ti-pi* through an opening specially made for this purpose. No sooner does he land when the ropes fly off still in knots, then is thrown outside the *ti-pi* among the crowd. This medicine man preferred to be left outside of the *ti-pi* to allow the grandfathers (spirit guides) to translate him inside. He'd be there one minute and in a split second he would be inside. This is witchcraft at its best.

This is what the medicine man was doing. While this is done, some of the people at this time can ask questions to the spirits – questions that no human can accurately answer, or where a human can only guess. If you feel that a curse was spoken on a relative, you can ask if it was a curse, and if it is, why, what caused them to do this, etc. – just whatever the situation that needs answering.

Anyway, my sister was among the people observing, sitting around near the *ti-pi* listening to the goings on. My sister said to me that she didn't believe a thing about what this man was doing. In fact, she opposed this man so much that she told the people there, "What do you think you are doing? This man is taking you for a ride. He is only after your finances. Can't you see that?"

She said this because the people there were giving this man huge amounts of money and gifts. Each person even if they were single still put in his/her share. This medicine man didn't have to lift a single finger to work, and he was earning more wages than all of them put together. She also told the people, "This man is not God. How could you treat him like he is?"

And then from the inside, she heard one of the spirits talking, saying 'This woman doesn't believe. Let's play a trick on her.' Just then a rattle came out of nowhere and bounced right off her head. The people around her were all terrified. They all stared at her with a horrified look with fear in their eyes. It happened so suddenly her mind didn't have time to react. She said that she didn't feel any effects from that incident.

But just before spring breakup where the winter roads are closed for the summer, Mom and Dad came to pick her up. She told me that I was also along, but I was only three or four years old. They came to take her back from the man she was staying with, because they felt she was too young yet to be with a man. Five years later our parents allowed my sister back with the same man when she turned eighteen. It sort of jarred my memory when she described the setting of the lumber camp. I was certain I saw it, but it was like a dream.

It was during the late spring sometime in the end of May or the beginning of June when my parents decided to go willow picket cutting. These are diamond willows cut into seven feet in length and sold to local buyers that freight them by train. Here on the reservation you lived in log shacks throughout the winter months and moved into tents during the spring until late autumn before the snow. It is a mobile home carried by team horses. You just throw all of your belongings in the tent, stove and stove pipes into the wagon box and away you go to your new location.

There is a little lake in the back of our place called Horse Lake. There used to be a lot of hay around that lake and each family had a section of hay field belonging to the families traditionally. Most time during haying season you would find families of people living along that lake haying for their livestock. This is where they set up their camp until these certain size of willows were cleaned out of the area. At least a quarter of a mile radius around their camp, Mom and Dad went out scouting for the best spots to start their project, and my sister was home alone. According to what she told me, our grandmother, my mother's aunt raised her as an adopted child, since Mom was also my grandmother's sister's child. They were camped there fifty yards or so further into the bush because Mom and Dad set up their camp in the open area along the bush line. My grandmother after raising my mom took on another child to raise who was my uncle's daughter (Mom's full brother). After my grandfather who helped raise my mom died, my grandmother never took another husband. She lived with her adopted child.

My sister said that she was preparing to make some dough in a bowl inside the tent to bake bannock outside. She walked outside with the bowl in hand toward the fireplace. That's when it happened. All of a sudden above that little lake she heard a ritual song. The man singing was that medicine man that she opposed. She heard that song sung all winter by that medicine man. It was the same voice. It was only then that she realized this medicine man possessed strange powers. Only then did fear hit her.

She said she screamed and threw that bowl away and ran as fast as she could to grandmother's tent and told her what just happened. Grandmother prayed for her and consoled her and encouraged her that nothing is going to happen to her, but that's when her problems started.

ANOTHER NOTE: Medicine men have their own spirit-given songs. It is not allowed to use another medicine man's song unless you earn it by being a helper to the medicine man for years, or passed down to you by a medicine man or bought through gifts. The only time these songs can be sung without the permission of the medicine man is at a sundance when the day of singing is done. Then the nighttime singers come on. Young and old alike can sing, just a fun time and also the daytime dancers get to rest. A substitute dancer is selected by the daytime dancer to dance for them during the nighttime. You can even disguise yourself during the night dancing like wearing a Halloween costume, something to that effect as not to be recognized. They painted up their faces, some wore handkerchiefs over their nose and mouth. The girls are different when they are night dancing. Well, maybe you can call it disguising because they really look pretty. They also painted their faces by putting on a lot of makeup. They color their cheeks and lips red or rosy. They powdered their faces, wore beaded headbands, etc. Ninety-nine per cent of the girls those days never wore makeup so this is why I said, 'you could call it disguise', and the nighttime dancers subtlely disappear one by one when dawn slowly approaches.

All of a sudden you will notice no one is dancing. A lot of times you wouldn't know who the man was that danced all night because all of a sudden as fast as he appeared from the shadows, he disappeared too. The night singers continue to sing without the nighttime dancers until they are told to stop by one of the sundance maker's helpers that are also chosen especially. After he stops the singers, he goes outside and starts walking around the sundance structure calling everyone to wake up. It is daylight when he makes one trip right around calling everyone to wake up. Then he comes inside and does the same.

He doesn't call, though. He's given a staff that he carries throughout the duration of the sundance. With that long staff he starts nudging the dancers to wake up also. After fifteen minutes or so, he'll repeat making another round. But at this time he will call out by saying, "Get up. It's time to start the day."

A half hour later he'll make another round, only this is the final time, so he carries an old pail, goes door to door even if you are outside making tea and such, he'll stop at the door of your tent, starts banging that pail with a stick and hitting the tent, saying, "Get up," and on he goes until every tent has been visited. That's how it used to be when I was a teenager. I don't know if that tradition is done today. Even at the time I excommunicated myself and renounced my traditional practices of witchcraft and did away with practicing the Indian religion, many of the traditional practices of the sundance were gone.

There will be a long silence while the dancers get prepared for the day and the sundance makers' helpers prepare their chosen task. Then you'll hear the eagle bone whistles blowing from the dancers – a signal they are ready. The sundance maker will kick off the day with his songs and from that time on throughout the day medicine men after medicine men are called to come and sing.

While my sister was telling me about her ordeal with this curse by this medicine man, she started telling me another story about the same medicine man. Apparently my mom actually told my sister about two well-known medicine men, one named Crow, and the other was the one who put the curse on my sister.

Some medicine men got together to make a ritual especially to call up to consult the dead, just like in Bible times in 1 Samuel 28:7:

> *"When Saul tricked the woman with the familiar spirit to call up Samuel"*

The ones waiting for the Lake of Fire are still in Hell, as mentioned in Luke 16:23-26:

> *"And in hell he lift up his eyes, being in torments, and seeth Abraham afar off, and Lazarus in his bosom. And he cried and said, 'Father Abraham, have mercy on me, and send Lazarus, that he may dip the tip of his finger in water, and cool my tongue for I am tormented in this flame.' But Abraham said, Son, remember that thou in thy lifetime receivedst thy good things, and likewise Lazarus evil things: but now he is comforted, and thou art tormented. And beside all this, between us and you there is a great gulf fixed: so that they which would pass from hence to you cannot; neither can they pass to us, that would come from thence."*

In Luke 23:43 it states:

> *"And Jesus said unto him, Verily I say unto thee, Today shalt thou be with me in paradise."*

In Matthew 27:50-53 it states:

> *"Jesus, when he had cried again with a loud voice, yielded up the ghost. And behold, the veil of the temple was rent in twain from the top to the bottom; and earth did quake, and the rocks*

> *rent; And the graves were opened; and many bodies of the saints which slept arose, And come out of the graves after his resurrection, and went into the holy city, and appeared unto many."*

After both of the medicine men were called up from the dead, the medicine man named Crow was the first one they consulted. He told the people there 'What we did while we were on earth was no good. It was wrong.' That's all he said. The other medicine man couldn't even talk, he just cried and cried without saying a word.

I was telling my wife that my mom must have told me this story, as I sort of recalled it vaguely. I blocked it out because I was very heavy into Indian religion, and that's not what I wanted to hear at that time. It was a discouragement to me when I was practicing it, so I just shut out the thought of it.

After toiling in preparing the structure in great anticipation of all sorts of revelations from these two dead medicine men's spirits, they only got those few words that Crow uttered. To hear it today was different, because it's a re-enforcement to what I've been saying all along: "There is no salvation in the Indian religion. Only through Christ Jesus can you get to the Father."

Approximately a week and a half after my sister disclosed this story to me, my wife Mary Ann and I did deliverance work on my sister. After we were done praying, God did a miraculous work on her. She said, "My head feels so light and clear. I used to be so groggy and my eyelids used to feel so heavy. My heart doesn't even ache any more. All of my sicknesses are gone!"

PROVOKE NOT

Many times my mother told me stories of the bad and hard times that she had to endure during her preteen and teenage years. That's when she was given away to marry a man. She was just a child who had no experience with how adults live together as man and wife. She was too young and naïve.

I remember how she used to laugh at herself when she told me stories of those early years when she was just a child, yet she already had a full grown man as her husband.

She'd talk about the times when she would be playing with children her age when she should have been preparing a meal for her husband who was out working. She used to tell me that many times my dad would find her with children her age, playing around and having fun. Then my dad would take a switch after her, sending her back to the place where they lived. These are the times she used to laugh at the situation that she put herself in, being too young and how naïve she was.

I am writing this part of my mother's life because these stories started something to explode inside of me that stayed with me that really set the course of my life in the way that I lived.

> *Visiting the iniquities of the fathers upon the children.*[44]

---

[44] Exodus 20:5

I know that there must be a lot of people out there that had the same impact that these stories had on me.

The hard times actually started after she had children. That's when the physical abuse began.

Her uncle and aunt that fostered her had a boy her age that she used to play with. They were like brother and sister. One day he got injured while they were out sliding on a steep hill during the winter. She was sure it was a severe spinal injury. She used to say that he never recovered from that injury, and at the end it took his life.

Life in her foster parents completely took a drastic turn. They went into total depression with heartbreak and sorrow. Life as she knew it with them was gone. Her uncle and aunt grieved night and day for their loss. It was during that time when she felt so sorry for the grieving foster parents. She felt compelled to do something, and that caused her life of physical abuse later in life.

One day she felt so bad for her grief stricken foster parents that she put her arms around them and made a solemn promise to them. "In the future when I start having children, if I conceive and it's a boy, I will make sure that I give him to you to raise as your own. But under one condition – that you stop grieving."

To her surprise, they both stopped mourning and grieving for the loss of their only son. When Mom conceived and had her first child, lo and behold, it was a boy. She kept that promise that she made and turned over her child to her foster parents.

My father went into a frenzy. He couldn't believe what my mother did. My father couldn't contain his anger. My mother would paraphrase what her husband accused her with. She used to say the words my father used to get his point across of how foolish my mother was by giving up her first child. 'What do you think my son is? Is he a dog that you just give away?' That was when my dad would strike her. At first it was one punch to remind her how angry my dad was. That one punch escalated gradually to two or three punches, and then full-blown physical abuse.

She started having other children. She had two wonderful boys in a row. By this time, my father had lost control of himself. He couldn't stop himself in beating my mother. My dad was about 5'5" tall and weighed about 140 pounds, if that. Yet when he'd be beating my mom, he acted like he was 6'5", 240 and bullet proof.

My mom would go into detail to describe the terrible beatings she received by my father's hand – how her face was black and blue and her eyes were swollen shut. She had just slits and she couldn't see out of them. She said that he drug my mom around by her hair while punching and kicking her. He acted so macho, beating on a woman that was helpless. I used to grind my teeth with folded fists. Rage erupted inside. I said to myself, 'Wait, just wait until I grow up. Boy, oh boy, he is going to wish he hadn't done that to my mom.'

Sometimes he also turned on my poor little brothers. She told me she saw my second oldest brother get beaten while he had him by one leg upside down. He held him this way while he beat him with a stick, not a switch. She was totally helpless. She couldn't do anything to defend my brother.

After he had done this, he would abandon them without provisions, to starve them. Another time my dad disappeared for a month or so, out womanizing. Again he had abandoned them without provisions.

When he finally returned, he found my mom living by herself with the boys on meager essentials just barely surviving. My mom told me stories of the sad state she endured with my older brothers. She said at times she'd go and pick scraps of clothing that people threw away where they had been camping in tents. She re-shaped them to my brothers' sizes to sew them for clothes they could wear when they went back to residential school in St. Albert, Alberta.

I would be all choked up with sadness. Then my dad had a right to come in and physically abuse them? Man, if that don't cause you to anger, I don't know what will. That part of her story got me angrier with my dad.

My uncle, my mom's full brother, happened to drop by during my dad's routine workout, beating on my mom. My uncle got so mad that he totally went into a rage, grabbed my dad and tore him off my mom and threw him to the ground. He challenged my dad into a man to man eye-gouging drug-out slugfest. My uncle called my dad down using every lowdown derogatory word he could find in his vocabulary. My dad just cowered. The way my mom described him was "like a dog with his tail tucked between his hind legs," and then my dad ran away. The only thing my uncle got that day was probably the fastest foot race he ever encountered in his life while he was trying to catch my dad.

It was right at this point of her story while she was reminiscing this awful scenario that I started feeling anger, rage, vengeance, and murder coming on inside of me toward my father – how I used to wish that I was all grown-up so that I could give him the same kind of beating that he gave to my mother, plus more. Maybe even kill him. In my mind a person that beat up women and children the way my father did had no right to live. I became a murderer in my heart by these terrible events that took place in my mother's life. Just think I was just a child, and already murder was instilled in my heart.

> *"And, ye fathers, provoke not your children to wrath."*[45]

This Scripture describes what could happen at the very beginning of your life.

---

[45] Ephesians 6:4

From that time on, I waited for that day when I will avenge for my mom's tormentor, who was my dad. By the time I grew up he was an old man, and so many different turn of events happened during that time when I heard my mom's stories to the time I grew up. My dad must have felt sorry for what he'd done to my brothers, because he spoiled me rotten.

That powerful urge to kill him subsided when the time came to avenge my mother. But that spirit of murder was still there, and it stayed dormant. Instead, I took it out on other people. It didn't take much for me to explode because that murderous spirit was there to thrust me into battle.

I told you how my mom fed me the brains of a muskrat just to test out a belief, where it is believed if a young child eats the brain, he or she will become as vicious as a muskrat. Well, it was true. By telling her story, my mom added murder to that belief. To top it all off, the medicine men and women fueled an already destructive person into a total monster by telling me the stories of how my ancestors were treated by the hands of the White Man, where they were considered more like animals than human beings, how they gradually stripped my people of all of their right to live, how my people were massacred, slaughtered women and children and how they hung and shot the Indian men at random. Just for spite and fun they starved many by withholding rations and many more died of sickness brought on by the White Man. They had no conscience.

When they were through with me, I was left with rebellion, vengeance, hatred and murder in my heart. They were like putting together a weapon of mass destruction. This was all stored up inside at a very young age. It was only by the grace of God that I didn't get in deeper trouble than I did. I give God all of the glory for pulling me through. Today I believe what He said in His Word, "*Vengeance is Mine.*"

This is my story. I know there must be many out there with almost identical feelings caused from different encounters just as bad or worse as what I experienced. But always remember, there is a way out, given to us by God through His Son Jesus Christ.

Here is another story to continue another early influence that led me on the wrong track. After Mom and Dad were separated, Mom brought me up. We lived alone in abandoned shacks on the reservation. Mom would clean them up and restore whatever she could and we'd live in them. I experienced something I was ashamed of telling, but it explains what the Scripture means when it states,

> *"Visiting the iniquities of the fathers upon their children"*

At that very young age I witnessed married men visiting my mother during the late night hours. I didn't know they were married men at the time, but later on in life I met these same men that I recognized as having a wife and children. From that time on, I started thinking in my mind that it was alright to do what I had witnessed at a very early age. I followed these men's footsteps right until I met Christ. It was only then that I found out that God forbade these actions, that it was a sin to commit adultery.

MOM'S BLESSING

Some of the stories my mother told me were not all doom and gloom. There were times in her beginning adolescent years when she mentioned God. She would say '*waka*' ('God' in Nakota) heard my cries and prayers. Once again she said my father left my mother to go out womanizing. She was left to fend for herself with almost nothing for food. It didn't take long when they had nothing left to eat.

Although she sort of knew that my father would not return, still, they waited for a couple of days for him to return. But to no avail, my brothers and sister were crying from hunger. This was early spring when the ice was still on the lake. She knew she had to do something, or they were going to fall prey to starvation.

But that day her mind was racing, searching for something that will bring food for her, my brothers and sister. At the same time she was asking *waka* for help when she saw these traps my father had left hanging on a limb of a medium-sized aspen tree that we call white poplar. She immediately knew there was hope for a possibility of getting something with these traps. She selected two of the traps and decided to venture out to the lake, she said.

Two traps were all she can handle besides the three small children to tend to at the same time. Two of my brothers could walk but they were very slow. She said she had to pack my sister on her back with a blanket tied around her body. She got on the ice and started walking along the bulrushes about fifty yards from shore.

Suddenly she decided just on an impulse to look down around one of the bulrushes. One of them created a large hole through the ice from the wind moving the bulrushes during the warm days of spring. What she saw was a feeding place for muskrats just under the ice. Right away she set my sister down on the blanket she used to carry her with. She got her little hatchet out and proceeded to chop the ice around that bulrush where she saw the feeding place. She made a hole big enough to fit her trap through. She said that she opened the trap's jaws and got the trap ready. She took her coat off and rolled up the sleeves of her sweater, got the trap by the handle and slowly pushed the trap to that feeding spot. While she was wiggling the trap to make it balance the trap, when it snapped shut. She must have touched something to trigger the trap, so she decided to pull it out and reset it. When she pulled the trap out, along came this big muskrat caught in the trap.

She said she got so startled that she threw the trap and the muskrat went tumbling on the ice. The she hit it with the hatchet handle and killed it. She said she was sure that it was God's doings and she gave praise and honor to *waka* for saving them from starvation.

She used to tell me of how close to *waka* she was in those days. She used to talk to *waka* every day, and not just short prayers but almost constantly. She later abandoned all of this intimacy with God after she separated with my father.

I was already born then and she told me that she got all dressed up and walked to church for Sunday Mass. When she got there she was met at the church door by the priest. The priest said to her, "You have no right to be here. I cannot allow you to defile my church. You have dishonored God by separating from your husband. You have committed an unpardonable sin. You are excommunicated from the Roman Catholic Church."

From that time on she felt her soul was condemned for hell. Her entire walk in life changed. She didn't see any sense in continuing her intimacy with *waka*. She turned to the way that leads to destruction.

NOTE: Before Adolph's mother died, she accepted the Lord and she is in Heaven serving the Lord. Adolph was sad on hearing of his mother's passing, but it gave him peace to know that his mother was there waiting for him to join her there.

THE PLOY

The Word of God states "Be not deceived. God is not mocked." Many changes happen when you come to Christ. Instead of bingos, casinos, horse races, dances, powwows, etc., you can't seem to get enough of going to church the first six months after coming to Christ. Our church was a big church we used to attend called Faith Cathedral in Edmonton, Alberta, Canada. It was there I first saw these two brothers in Christ that had sort of a mixed impact on my walk with Christ. You could call it a lesson. They were both song leaders in that church. One brother was White; the other brother was Indian. You could tell they had been playing music together in the way they backed each other's singing.

I was just starting my walk with Christ. Gosh, I was impressed and blessed at the same time. I used to wonder if I'll ever be in front of a huge congregation like them one day. They were like celebrities to me at the time, because they seemed separate from the rest of the congregation. They were always up in front and together. I held them in high regard, not knowing that they too were human like me.

As a beginner my mind was altogether different than today. Not realizing that I had put them on a pedestal, I even had this thought that maybe because of their spiritual insight that they could see through me. Crazy thoughts like that would surface in my mind. I even though, 'I wonder if I am worthy to even shake their hand', seeing that I just started in Christianity. I didn't know at the time that one day one of them was even going to support the ministry that God gave me.

Those were the days of excitement, jubilation in the Lord. Everything was a new experience – revelation after revelation of a brand new life in God's Holy Spirit.

As time went on, I got to meet both of the brothers at a different meeting place. Eventually a sister in Christ managed to rent a much smaller space but big enough to hold a couple of hundred people. It was located in another area of the same building where the Indian brothers and sisters congregated for revivals. This is where I finally got to shake hands with these two brothers. That was when I finally realized that these brothers were no different than I was.

We were in the same boat together as the ministry God gave me grew with leaps and bounds. No one was ever bold enough to renounce the Indian religion quite like the way that I did. Because of my involvement in the Indian religion for thirty-seven years, I knew it led to nowhere but in a circle. I told it to my Indian people the way that the Indian religion is. I didn't back down or become a coward because its lies almost brought me to hell. That is exactly where I would have ended up if Jesus didn't intervene and heal me.

As the first couple of years went by, I got to know these brothers a whole lot more. I found out one of the brothers had left and divorced his first wife, whom every Christian brother and sister swore that she was a devout born again Christian. When I confronted this brother about his first wife, he flatly denied that she was ever a Christian. He told me that his first wife professed to be a Christian, but she actually was involved in the New Age Movement, and that he doesn't recommend that as a Christian group.

I didn't pursue it any further because it looked like a game, and I probably would never know who was telling the truth. Only God knew the truth, and only at the time of judgment will it ever be revealed who was telling the truth. I left it at that. I also eventually found out the White brother's wife was an Indian, and a very devout born-again Christian woman.

But guess what happened? After a few years of supporting the ministry that God gave me, this White brother moved to another province (in case you readers are from the U.S.A., a province is like a state). Why I am saying this is because I have been ministering in the United States. I came across people that don't care to know about other countries like Canada, so you might wonder what I am talking about.

I received a letter from this White brother who left his phone number for me to phone him pronto. As soon as I got the message, I phoned and he told me, "You got to come down here. People here really need deliverance. I've been ministering in song on these small reservations. There are all kinds of demonic activities."

So my late wife with our children all ended up going there. After spending the summer there, we came back. One day a few years later I received this phone call from him by surprise.

He said, "I'm back in town. Come and visit. I am doing real good on a new business venture. I got a new house, motor home – the whole nine yards."

He gave me his address, so away I went. In fact, I was very happy for him. He deserved this blessing, because I was completely in the dark to what this brother had done to receive this blessing. To me, I envisioned him as when I last saw him with his first wife. I didn't anticipate what I was going to encounter. When we got to the address he gave me, there were these children – total strangers to me – playing in the yard. It couldn't be his children. They were too young, either that, or they were the neighbor's kids.

In any case, he must have been watching out for my arrival because the White brother came out of this beautiful house to greet us.

I went inside and sat down. From the other room came this beautiful young woman. The brother said to me with a smile from ear to ear, “Meet my new wife!”

I was in complete shock. I thought to myself, ‘This can’t be happening. This just can’t be real. The brother knows better. He couldn’t switch wives. This is not Christian at all. This is bad fruit.’ But as bad as it was, it was real.

I found out real quick that not only was this White brother’s new wife pretty, but she was a smart business woman. She was the one who set up this business that the White brother was boasting about. Plus, this pretty woman had three or four children of her own from her previous husband. These were the children that I first saw playing in the yard, plus the this White brother managed a child with her – a boy approximately four years old by the time I had this contact with this White brother.

Anyway, I didn’t know what to make of it. I really had mixed emotions. I also felt scared from the fear of the Lord. I think it was because I held this White brother in high regard all of these years. He had done so much for me supporting the ministry that God gave me. What he did didn’t fool me one bit. Does he really think he’s fooling God? I mean, to me this is SIN and hypocrisy. Sin can never enter into heaven. Plus, he flushed that powerful testimony he had down the drain.

The thing that scared me was the fact that he acted as if he had done nothing wrong. He had no fear of God or reverence. Was this brother even real? Was he just playing church all along? If that’s the case, just how many of them are out there anyway?

Then about a year later again he phoned me and says, “I am almost your next door neighbor. I am only a couple of miles away from you. Come down and visit. He had moved to the country.”

After he moved, bad, bad things started happening for the brother, but first I would like to clarify what caused this brother to leave his first wife. Yes, you guessed it. He followed what his song leading brother in Christ did. This brother probably knew exactly what the other brother did to leave his first wife. They were very close. He knows more than what I heard.

Anyway, this is the story I heard after we finished ministering and came back from where this brother moved. He met this beautiful woman during his ministry, which caused the enemy to enter into this brother's life. This thought probably has been sitting dormant since the other brother left his first wife years before. It just now was activated when he first laid eyes on that beautiful woman.

In order to cause his first wife to leave him, this brother started drinking. I remember my late wife telling me what this brother's first wife used to tell her about how mean and abusive her husband was. He would beat her body black and blue, although her faced showed no marks of abuse. I remember while we were visiting this brother and his first wife. They both went upstairs. About ten minutes later they came down. This sister told my wife during those ten minutes her husband was beating her with his fist on the body. When they came back down, the brother had a smile on his face and talking as if everything was normal, like nothing happened.

When I heard the brother started drinking, oh man, this compassion for the sister came over me. If the brother was abusive while cold sober, he must have turned into a monster while under the influence of alcohol. Just imagine the uncontrollable beatings he must have inflicted upon his wife. No wonder I heard it didn't take long for the brother to get his divorce.

When he got his divorce papers, he immediately sobered up and straightened his life out because the drinking was a ploy to get a divorce. Now that he got that out of the way, he proceeded in courting this beautiful woman that he was now married to.

Approximately one year later, I was suffering and struggling, battling my way back from a severe fall from my walk (that I wrote in my first book). I was almost one year in my recovery. There is a very small town two miles north of my place on the Reservation. My brother-in-law and I were walking to where we Reservation people pick up their mail. We were in no hurry. We were just passing the time. We were just dragging along, slowly walking and talking about nothing in particular. We spoke of many funny stories of things that happened to us and others, past and present, when we met this brand new van.

It stopped, and behind the wheel was this White brother who had it made. He told me he went on a business trip over the long weekend by himself. When he got back to his house, he found three police cars parked at his place and a couple of big U-haul trucks ready to go standing there. His wife and stepchildren were under police protection. He told me that he got a chance to grab his son away from her, but the big policeman ripped his son away from him. He said that the policemen almost drew their guns on him.

He tried to entice me into going back into witchcraft to bring his second wife back. He was going to pay me a very large sum of money if I would do it. The devil knew when to bring this offer to me. Like I said, I was at a very weak state as far as spirituality was concerned, but I still had my senses with me.

I told him, "It's extremely tempting, very hard to resist but I have to pass. I fell deep enough into sin with alcohol. I cannot get myself to go deeper by accepting your offer. There are many medicine men and women here on this reservation."

Just then my brother-in-law spoke up and asked, "What does he want?" in Nakota Sioux. I told him but before my brother-in-law got a chance to talk to this White brother, I quickly told this supposedly brother, you saw what the Lord did during my ministering. I said I wasn't in no wise playing church. I was for real. I am still for real depending on God to bring me through this valley. You have to ask someone else."

Then he asked me, "You must know someone." Just then my brother-in-law cut into our conversation and asked him, "What is it you need?"

I know my brother-in-law had what he was looking for, but I wasn't going to acknowledge that. In the end this supposedly brother got what he was looking for from my brother-in-law. This supposedly brother had all of the items needed to bring her mind into subjection. He even had some of her hair from her hairbrush. I don't know what had taken place from this ordeal if he got her back and lost her again. I can't say.

All I know is approximately three years after this incident he came back to my place looking for my brother-in-law with a picture of another woman. I was already recovered from my bout with alcohol and well on my way with God again when I last saw him. I never saw him or heard of his whereabouts since then. Like I said from the beginning, this was a huge lesson.

> *"For he that soweth to his flesh shall of the flesh reap corruption."*[46]

When I look in the Scriptures to find something to support what this brother had done, I just couldn't find any Scriptures on marriage and divorce. Actually what I found in the Scriptures was totally against what this brother did. Of course, history repeats itself again. King David did the same thing and lost everything.

I found one Scripture that covers it all:

---

[46] Galatians 6:8

"Not every one that saith unto me, Lord, Lord, shall enter into the kingdom of heaven; but he that doeth the will of My Father which is in heaven."[47]

[47] Matthew 7:21

MY COUSIN

What I am about to disclose happened during the latter part of the 1950's. This story is about one of my many cousins that I have. This particular cousin was always a loner, and to make life tougher he didn't have much schooling, probably grade 4 or 5, if that. But he survived by hard work.

One thing he was good at was hunting and trapping. Other than that he hired out as a farm hand during the summer months. Good thing he had a strong back and a will to survive. This part probably relates to a lot of people in those days and maybe even now.

This story is not totally about his hard work ethics. It is actually about a one-time incident that happened to him. It was during mid winter when this story took place. There is an area west of our reservation, approximately sixty miles, where half of our people on our reservation have their traplines given to them by the Government to provide sustenance and finances through trapping fur-bearing animals.

My cousin was one of them, and he made good use of it during trapping season. One day he came to the town called Whitecourt to sell some of his furs to get himself some supplies and provisions that he needed. After he sold his furs, he was walking around town when without a warning a police car pulled up and parked just ahead of the direction he was walking. The policeman got out and waited for him.

When he got to where the policeman was, the officer asked him, "What is your name?"

And, of course, without hesitation he told him his name not knowing why the policeman wanted to know. The policeman replied, "Well, Mister (naming him), you are under arrest."

My cousin was caught totally unawares, because as long as he knew he couldn't ever remember breaking the law. He asked, "What for?"

The policeman said, "I'll tell you once we get to the station." When they got there, he got his summons. The charge was uttering and forging documents. My cousin was totally dumbfounded, because he hadn't left his trapline since late fall when winter trapping season started.

He found out this cheque that was forged was cashed while he was on his trapline. Although they let him go on his own recognizance, he had to come to court for this charge. The court case drug out for at least a year.

What had happened was someone fitting my cousin's description had forged and cashed this cheque. In those days this charge could get you at least a year in prison if you got convicted. A lot has changed in the justice system from this time in the 1950's until today in 2008, fifty some-odd years later. If this thing happened today, my cousin would have gotten a slap on the wrist and he would have had to sweep sidewalks for a couple of hours if he got convicted.

The store owner saw my cousin through the store window and he called the police and told them, "The Indian who forged that cheque I cashed is in town. I just saw him walking down the street." That was why the police picked him up.

I heard this talk about the court case when I was a young kid. Because my cousin knew that he wasn't the man that did this, he fought the case. He couldn't prove his innocence because he had no witness to prove that he had been on his trapline at the time this cheque was cashed. It was his word against the store owner. Like I said, he didn't have the smarts to forge anything. Still, I heard talk how he must have done it. All sorts of murmuring was going on. Some said he probably collaborated with someone that knew how to forge, etc. blah, blah, blah.

To prove his point, my cousin got my uncle who we cousins called "Big Unc". Through him they searched out a medicine man that could astro travel. They hired him and did a ritual to find the man that did it.

Big Unc was always involved in witchcraft as long as I can remember, always professing in having spiritual powers, but one thing he did not possess was clairvoyance or astro traveling. I remember he always boasted about his powers and he used it to cause fear in people when he got upset.

I happened to be pretty close to him. I saw him several times when he got offended. Big Unc was my uncle from my mother's side of the family. At one time a cousin from my dad's side of the family got Big Unc mad. I heard Big Unc telling him, "You better be very careful in the way you live from now on, because you are going to notice a change on your face. So don't push it, or else! Not only am I going to turn your face jet black but your mouth is also going to be twisted to the side of your face!"

Although my cousin was inebriated at the time he got my uncle mad, it created quite an impact on my cousin. We lived just across from where my cousin lived, so a couple of days later I went over there to see if he was in. He was, and it didn't take long before the subject was about my uncle who threatened him. He must have been rattled to his boots. He was talking about it with fear in his voice.

Foolishly, he said, "If anything happens to me, I will kill him by shooting him with a gun." My cousin knew that he had no one to turn to. He was never raised in the beliefs of the spirit world, but he wasn't totally naïve about it. He just wasn't interested.

He was too engulfed in sports. If it was today, he probably would have no problem in making any of the junior hockey teams. He was a one-in-a-million hockey player. He was a fanatic consumed in the world of hockey. Once he was on the ice, no one could touch him. He would rather skate and practice than eat, skating circles pails and tin cans placed on the ice, stick handling around them all day. Then after supper he'd go out again until it was so dark that you couldn't see the puck any more. Skating was so natural to him that it was effortless.

A lot of times throughout the winter months, I spent time with him. He made me put on a pair of skates, and he took me out to this pond that they lived by. He'd have me skating, and he would make me play hockey with him. The only way I got to handle the puck was if he would give it to me. Otherwise I couldn't get it away from him. He'd be skating circles around me. Sometimes when he got too close to me, I'd just grab him and hang on and he would be dragging me around until I let go.

Like many Indians, his downfall was alcohol. Although he was in first stages of life in a world of alcoholism, he was hooked already. It wasn't until his father died that life actually changed dramatically for him, and to think he was only sixteen. It just seemed he lost all interest he had in everything. He threw it out the window and walked away.

Until that day, you would find him home (being the youngest in the family) taking care of his parents whenever he was needed. I remember during the summer months there used to be a lot of sporting events happening in the towns around our reservation where our baseball teams were invited to play in tournaments. My cousin would catch a ride with someone and find his way there. He would join the foot races because he was a very fast runner. He would make his lunch money that way and enjoy himself.

The day he left the reservation he left whatever life he had, never looking back. He ended up in the back alleys of the City of Edmonton on Skid Row. This is where he spent the rest of his life. Before all of this took place, his life didn't look so bleak. There was a possibility that he was contemplating in starting a family of his own at one point. All of that took a drastic change when his dad died. Everything just seemed to shatter and dissolve into thin air. Somehow he stayed away from committing suicide and he chose instead the long suffering of life being a rubbie on Skid Row. He threw the gift away that God gave him to become one of the few that made it in big time sports in hockey. Even as of right now as I am writing this story, I have been witnessing young Indian hockey players with real potential, who are very skillful fall right, left and centre to alcohol, drugs and young girls. I am positive you would have seen a whole lot of Indian hockey players in the NHL, if they would only sacrifice their good times and get serious. Very few Indian boys pass that barrier of alcohol, drugs and girls.

Why do I say "girls"? Well, these young adolescent Indian males get to shack up too soon, right at the point when they are excelling in their chosen sport of hockey. Once that happens, you can't get them to go to a faraway city to hone their skills. They eventually fall prey to alcohol and drugs.

As an older person I have seen the behavior those young people go through. They get blinded by infatuation. They overlook the reality of so many mature facts; they dive into a relationship only to regret it later.

Anyway, around 1975 or 1976 after I'd been sober for a couple of years, word came to us that my cousin hung himself in prison. Prison guards found him hanging in the washroom. They cut him down too late. He already sustained a broken neck. He was kept alive for 48 hours in a hospital near the prison, but no one went to see him, even when his family was asked to go see him alive for the last time.

Big Unc didn't last as long. He also committed suicide around 1964. Why I remember it was 1964 is because I was working cutting pulpwood for Northwest Pulp and Power in Hinton, Alberta, during the winter. My cousin from my mother's side of the family and I boarded a train to come to pay our last respects. The train was non-stop to Edmonton. When we got to Edmonton, we met some of our people from the Reservation, so we asked about the funeral. They told us we were a day too late.

I remember Big Unc very well, who always carried a medicine pouch inside his shirt pocket whenever he was trapping or hunting. He always bragged about a couple of good friends he had that were considered powerful medicine men. He told stories of how they dared other medicine men to challenge them in a medicine war, where the other party backed down. He used to say he never was afraid of any medicine men knowing he had those two friends.

He told me stories of why he had to be with someone while out trapping or hunting. He said that the few times he went alone, he would encounter a spirit that would manifest in human form – a wicked old man that had a big Roman nose. His eye sockets looked like they were far back into his skull. He was short and skinny as a stick and it always had a pipe that he smoked. He'd show up at random late at night at his camp. (When you're out trapping usually you camp under a spruce tree that has the best shelter at the base of the tree, because it has the least snow or sometimes it is even bare underneath.)

He had a name for this spirit – "Pah-chooch". He used to tell me when this spirit shows up, you better be spiritually strong, or else you'll pass out. He will scatter all of your provisions, put out your fire, and it will go as far as strip off your clothes and leave you to die.

He would say to me, "I could never have a decent sleep. Sometimes I would have to battle this spirit all night long, like a battle of wits of spiritual knowledge. It could be like a card game to see who can outdo the other. Another thing is this spirit would disappear suddenly when daylight approached.

He only moves about during the night. Sometimes you can hear his spirit singing a handgame song, banging on what sounded like an old pail, always in the darkest low lying areas, like along the banks of a creek where the spruce trees are tall and thick or like a hollow where it's always dark. This is why I have to have a companion with me whenever I am out hunting or trapping. This is the only time that this spirit would leave me alone when I am with someone else."

One thing he warned me about this spirit is never to say bad thing concerning "Pah-chooch". "He will know you have been bad-mouthing him. Look out if he catches you camping out. I heard stories where someone was talking foolishly about this spirit. It happened to one of my uncles," he said. "Even though there were four of them in the group on their way to their traplines, the subject of the spirit came up."

'I hope it don't show up in our camp tonight,' one had said. Big Unc said to me, "One of them said, 'If he ever shows up, I'll show him a thing or two. I am going to grab him, hold him into a ball and put him in the fire', and he proceeded to laugh about it. They had walked all day and they were just preparing for bed after a meal when this guy said this.

When they got under the blankets he felt a shiver like a rush go through his body up to the back of his head. This guy who happened to be my mother's uncle who brought her up used to feel this way when this spirit was going to show up. He kind of shook his shoulders when he felt this. I guess he heard someone say, "pssh".

He looked toward the sound. Here sat that spirit on top of a pile of wood they had gathered for the night. He had one leg across the other with his elbow on top of his knee holding a pipe in his mouth, with a half grin on his face. His eyes focused on that man that was talking about him. That was the last he remembered until he woke up half frozen with the fire completely out. He was the only one that woke up, while the rest slept through this whole ordeal.

He had to restart the fire and drag on some dry logs before he went to sleep. Next day when they all got up, the guy that was talking against that spirit found that his pants and underwear were down to his knees. This spirit was known to humiliate anyone who spoke against him. The stories from the old timers are that this spirit was known to fondle and sexually assault you just for his own satisfaction of embarrassing and humiliating you, to get his last laugh.

I guess the rest of the guys there were really teasing their cousin when he complained of soreness on his privates and anal area. I guess one of them told him, “Don’t ever do that again. You almost got all of us frozen.”

My uncle, Big Unc, never followed through with his threat because my cousin’s face never turned black or twisted but one other thing happened to my cousin that same summer. Someone smashed a wine bottle on top of his head. The jagged end that was left on the neck of the bottle cut the side of his face down to his neck. It left a reminder of his start down the dark trail of alcohol abuse.

Now back to my first story: They had this ritual inside a cabin made out of lumber. This medicine man that Big Unc got for my cousin was inside a structure made from rails. These rails were jammed tightly from the floor to ceiling to form a circle wrapped in canvas. The medicine man would astro travel brought by the spirit guides when the medicine man was heard calling my cousin.

He said, “I found him. What do you want me to do with him? Should I bring him here?” I heard from Mom that Big Unc tried frantically urging my cousin to agree, but, still my cousin refused.

He said, “Just so long as my people know that I wasn’t lying. That’s all I care.”

Another thing was that it wasn’t going to help his court case, even if they brought the man there anyway. What court is going to believe this ever could happen? After a long hard battle in court, they couldn't find enough evidence to convict my cousin. If they had convicted him on the hearsay of that store owner, they would have convicted an innocent man.

This cousin eventually became a very powerful medicine man, whom all of my relatives highly respected and honored – all except me. I remember my sister using him in a court case many years later when my cousin was way up there in age.

My sister wasn't the accused on this trial that took place. She was the victim. She got savagely beaten and raped by three white men. Although my sister said there were more of them, she couldn't identify them all – only three. My sister kept going to court. It was when they finally reached the last trial day that is when my sister hired my cousin as insurance that these men that did this awful deed didn't get away.

I was there to witness this ceremony and the feast my sister did. It was done the day before the trial of these men. I wasn't saved at that time, so I was full of anger and vengeance. Even after these men were convicted if the security wasn't as tight as it was, I would have sucker punched one of them, even though that wouldn't make much of a difference since they were already convicted. To me it was personal to justify my feelings and then I would have been satisfied.

Sometimes, when I have been telling a story several times to different people I don't remember if I wrote this already or not. A lot of times I find I hadn't written it. Such is the case on the rest of this story of my cousin.

After years of smoking he got throat cancer. In the city there is a hospital where people go that are almost on their last breath. If the doctors at this hospital can't do anything there, then no other hospital can. This is the last stop for people in that condition.

One day in that hospital I was there to pick up some medication for my late wife. While I was waiting for her prescription to be filled, I met this man from our reservation that works there as a pipe carrier and medicine man. He visits people who believe in the Indian religion. I asked him if anyone was there that I knew.

He said, "Yes," and he mentioned my cousin and told me what floor and room that he was in. I went there and found my cousin sitting in a chair all hooked up with a plastic pipe inserted through his windpipe where the cancer had eaten a hole. He saw me and he nodded, like he was saying "Hi". I shook his hand. He couldn't talk, but he had a clipboard on his knees. He wrote something and handed me the clipboard. I looked on a sheet of paper that was on the board and it read, "Pray for me."

I was more than happy for asking me for prayer. This was a chance of a lifetime to me as a minister. This is what I wish that everyone would ask for, instead of trying to implement the gospel in ways that is not offensive. At times their lives depend on how you present Jesus to people.

I told him, "I am happy to pray with you." I kind of enlightened him on who Jesus Christ was, why God brought Him here on this earth before I led him in the Sinner's Prayer. After that I sat and talked to him.

I thought to myself, 'My work is done. My deed for the Lord is at least done for today'. But the Lord kept impressing in my spirit that I wasn't through praying. I kept answering back, 'But I did my work. What more?'

When the thought finally hit me, I was almost ready to leave. 'Oh yes, of course. He is a medicine man and he needs deliverance.'

I asked my cousin, "Can I pray for you one more time before I leave?" He nodded, so I laid my hands on his head and I started commanding those demons of witchcraft and sorcery to start leaving.

"I break your power and stronghold upon my cousin, in the Name of Jesus Christ by His shed Blood, let him go! All you ancestral spirits, let go of him right now!"

All of a sudden, my cousin started waving his arms. He was trying to knock my hand away. Manifestations of ancestral spirits and generations of strongholds were starting to break and loosen. Tears, snot and saliva and some foam were even bubbling around the area of the tube that was inserted into this throat.

Suddenly he stopped fighting to knock my hands away from having it on his head; his arms fell down limp on top of a little table that was put there over his lap. Also his head fell on the towels that were around his throat and neck area. He sat still with his eyes closed for approximately a full minute before he made any kind of movement.

I let him go and I watched him, observing if all was well. Then the first thing he did after he started to move again was to yawn. He opened his eyes again and he started yawning some more – a clear indication that the Lord totally delivered him. He got some tissue and wiped his eyes and blew his nose, got more tissue wiping his face and around his mouth.

Then he yawned some more. I asked him, "You're tired, aren't you?" He was moving his lips and I could read what he said, "I want to sleep" (in our own language). I said to him before I left, "You probably will be out of this hospital and be back on the reservation before I do, because I know for a fact that the Lord had touched you."

I was just visiting here in Edmonton and I would be leaving in a couple of days for the reservation also. Sure enough, when I got back I saw him walking on the road, like there was nothing wrong. I smiled to myself, knowing what the Lord can do. I never saw him after that time, ever again, but I know I will when I get home.

Although my cousin got a touch from the Lord, the cancer lingered to eventually bring down my cousin. Even when cancer may look victorious, we know it lost out because Jesus already had my cousin on the other side.

So my cousin not only made it back to the reservation before me, but also he made it home to that beautiful mansion before me.

Since then I go to hospitals witnessing to the sick with a 98 percent success rate (just counting the ones who are sick in hospitals). Jesus had been rejected flatly only twice. My wife and I even went twice to one of my first cousin's from my father's side of the family. My cousin was lying in bed dying of cancer of the pelvis. He had every kind of traditional relic hanging all around his bed, including the eagle feather and medicine bundle, with sweet grass burning and a statue of the Virgin Mary and rosary on his nightstand.

We just couldn't convince him to let us pray with him. The second time we went to see him he was a day and a night away from dying. Still he would not let go of the old ways. I could never forget the last words he used. He said, "Go and pray somewhere else." The next day he died.

DOOR TO DOOR

One time I got a call from a sister from northern Alberta. Something, she said, was attacking her. She said, "I heard about you through some Christian Indians that you had a ministry in deliverance, especially pertaining to the Indian religion, and they said you would be the one to contact after I told them my problem."

It was approximately a year after my first wife went home to be with Jesus. All I ever did was travel around, going to revival after revival. When she said she needed deliverance, I suggested, "If you pay for my gas, I can come down seeing I am not doing anything and there isn't any previous booking that I am obligated to. Otherwise I can pray for you over the phone if you can't."

She said, "But yes, I'll pay for your gas because after you pray for me, I'd like you to pray for my brother who is in a terrible state of illness."

It's about a six-hour drive from here, so I got there quite late, probably around 1 or 2 a.m. to the nearest town from where she lives. I still had to phone her when I got there so she could direct me to her home.

The next day we sat down and talked about this attack she was experiencing. Like any other Indian person, she had a long string of medicine men/women in her bloodline. She said that this force would attack her mind. She would get this sensation like a halo or a ring of pressure around her head and it seemed like this ring of pressure would spin around her head, although she tried earnestly to focus on other things to try not to let this force overtake her mind completely. Still she said sometimes this pressure and spinning would get so intense that she would get dizzy. She had to stop what she was doing and wait until this dizziness subsided. The thing comes and goes and it hits at random without a warning at anywhere. She said she was positive it was witchcraft. She never once in all her entire life had these symptoms. It came so suddenly from out of nowhere.

"I had never done anything to cause such torment to my mind. I got prayer for it several times, but still it just would not go away. I didn't know what to do. I even had tests done by doctors and nothing showed up. Until I heard of you and how you practiced the Indian religion before you came to Christ, and you knew what to do in these situations. This is why I felt I had to see you for this matter. I was more than happy to pay for your gas to come here."

After saying this, she asked, "So what do you think from what I disclosed so far?" I said, "It sure sounds like witchcraft. If it is, something will happen during my prayer or immediately after praying for you." Then I asked, "Are you ready, and if you are, we'll start."

She said, "I guess this is what I've been praying for to happen. I am ready."

I took my anointing oil and anointed her head. I felt her body jump like she sat on a sharp object. I quoted James 5:14, and I said, "I now anoint you with oil in the Mighty Name of Jesus Christ."

I proceeded in prayer with my hand on her forehead. Right away I felt a struggle that something was blocking and resisting my prayer. She wasn't receiving the anointing that was going through my hand. I felt a lot of pain in her heart, so I stopped and took my hand away and sat down.

She opened her eyes and a look of fear came upon her. She said, "What's wrong?"

I told her, "Oh nothing to fear about. The Holy Spirit just showed me that you have a lot of pain stored away in your heart. We have to deal with that first before I come against this curse of witchcraft."

She said to me, "Like what?" And I countered, "Like unforgiveness." She paraphrased and said, "Unforgiveness?"

I just nodded my head. She said, "I forgive everybody that ever harmed me in my life. I don't understand what you're telling me. Can you explain a little more?"

"Yes," I said, "You forgave everybody but yourself. You left yourself out."

She folded her arms and flopped back on the chair. She was sitting and staring without a word, biting and sort of chafing on her lower lip, like she was either dumbfound or thinking real hard on something. We sat silent for a minute before she spoke again.

She said, "That's the first time I ever heard of anyone saying that. Now you are gonna have to teach me on how to forgive myself."

"Okay," I said, "but we are going to be digging a lot of things from your past right from childhood from the first time you started remembering episodes in your life. Can you do that?" She said, "I think so." I told her, "What we are doing right now has a very vital part on your deliverance because we cannot leave an opening where the devil might use to stay. We have to shut all doors and then break the stronghold of that curse, and you have to continue to keep it closed because he is going to return to check you out again.[48]

He calls your body a house, and the body like a house has many doors and closets that need to be cleaned out and closed shut. If those doors are not closed, he comes and goes as he will please. For example, one door might be

[48] Matthew 12:44-45

jealousy, idolatry, another stealing, lying, murder in your heart, unforgiveness, hate, fornication, etc. Then I asked her, "Have you ever been in a residential school?"

She said, "Yes, but I was not abused at the residential school. It happened at home. I was physically and mentally abused at the residential school. All of the sexual abuse happened at home by my relatives but I have forgiven them already."

Then I asked her, "What happens to your emotions inside when you encounter face to face with one of them even after you had forgiven them?" She said, "I try not to, but it still has some sort of impact on me." "Like what?" I asked. She said, "Like they are no longer blood and their thoughts are evil which brings me back to what they did to me. Then I have to forgive all over again." I asked her again, "Why? Why do you feel you have to forgive again? Wasn't once enough?"

She said, "Because I feel like my heart is ready to explode with all kinds of mixed feelings once more." That's when I told her, "This is exactly what I am talking about when I say you haven't forgiven yourself. You see, you're the one that carrying all this pain, not them. They were probably satisfied and pleased themselves for what they did to you while you're dragging yourself down with all of this hatred, anger, murder, unforgiveness in your hear. You were tormenting your own self, hurting your own self. No one else was carrying this pain for you. You had it stored up. So in order to release all this pain, you need to forgive yourself."

There was one more thing in life that almost destroyed her was her husband that she loved since she was a young teenage girl. After she had children from him, he decided to leave. It totally broke her heart. Her life went into a shambles, scattered beyond repair. What really made it hard on her was the fact the children were grown. They were raised up together, and now that the hard part of child rearing was over when she should be really enjoying life together, he packed up and left her. Although I never heard his side of the story, still she had a lot of pain to deal with. I asked her, "Did you catch all of what I said?" She said,"Yes," so I said, "Shall we start on your deliverance?" She said, "Yes, I'm ready."

When the LORD was through with her, she could not believe the difference it made in her life. I give all the honor, glory and praise to Jesus for the awesome work He did.

After her deliverance, she brought me to her reservation approximately an hour and a half drive on a gravel road. When we got there, the first place she took me was to her sister's home where I ended up doing the process of deliverance. It seemed the whole family was brought up in the teaching of Indian spiritual beliefs. Until they recently turned to Christ Jesus, they finally could discern the difference. Then they realized they were under bondage from ancestral spirits that their family honored.

We had a small lunch, and during that time they told me about that their older brother was extremely ill. They were positive it wasn't all sickness. Most of it was due to curses.

Afterward one of the sisters brought me to her brother's house which was approximately a hundred yards further in the bush. In between this sister's house and their brother's house was a big old well-made log house. When we passed by that log house, I felt cold chills run through my body. There was an evil presence surrounding that log house. I didn't say anything, I just kept on walking.

We got to her brother's house. It was a one-room house just recently completed. Her brother was lying in his bed with a kerchief tied around his head. I found out one of the many problems was migraine headaches. That was why he had the kerchief tied around his head to sort of alleviate the pain of the condition this man was in. There was no way he should have been home by himself. He should have been in an intensive care unit in a hospital. His hair had fallen off. There were only patches of long hair here and there. He was frail and weak because he would shake when he forced himself to sit up.

They told me a medicine man had been coming around doctoring him but there was no improvement. That's been going on for about a year, the sister said. The sister introduced me to her brother and explained the purpose that I was there. She told him I was a minister who once practiced the Indian religion, that Jesus Christ set him from the bondage of witchcraft. It brought a smile upon his face, but I could tell it was from skepticism. I could see that it didn't set right with him when his sister said Indian religion was witchcraft.

You see, this man didn't have any schooling. His sister was interpreting for me, and she told me that a curse of death was spoken on him. The medicine man that was doctoring him seemed helpless against this curse. Although the medicine man tried everything from brewing medicines from mother earth to healing lodges (sweat lodge) to smudging the man sick man's body with many kinds of incense along with prayer and chanting, nothing worked. In fact, it seemed the sickness worsened.

Anyway, I asked if he would allow me to pray for him, and he agreed. I started asking him questions. The first one was, "Do you still practice the Indian religion?" He said, "Yes."

I told him that the Indian religion and God's Word contradict. It's got to be one way or it's no use even trying. "Are you willing to let go of Indian religion if a healing was going to take place?"

I guess he didn't fully understand, and he asked, "Like what?"

I asked him, "Do you still have your medicine bundle?" Again the answer was "Yes." "Do you have it here inside your house?"

He said, "No, it's stored away inside that old log cabin." I said to him,

"Then would you allow us to go and get it so that we can get rid of it?"

That last question almost took whatever little life he had left. He got all excited. He started talking loud and fast, waving his hands around. When he was through, I asked the sister, "What did he say?"

"He said, 'I'd rather go jump in the river and drown myself than to destroy my sacred medicine bundle.'"

I had to explain why it was important to do this. "You are carrying that medicine bundle, and it does no good and nothing for you, because it's the spirits that do all of the false lying wonders. As mere humans we don't have that kind of spiritual power. We are only helping those spirits in keeping us in bondage. Without humans they are also helpless, and that medicine bundle belongs to them. They have the right to be there and then we also give them that right by honoring them. Now, if we burn up that medicine bundle they have to go elsewhere because they have nothing to keep them here. Even if I kick those spirits out of your body by the shed blood of Jesus Christ, they will return because you never renounced your old Indian spiritual ways."

After explaining all of this, he still shook his head. I knew what he was thinking because I had gone through this before. The fear of these spirits is intense. It's terrifying. Just the thought of it makes you tremble and shudder. You are sure your life is over instantly. That is how deeply conditioned you are made by the strict teaching passed down by our ancestors.

Afterward the sister and I went back to the first house. We told the other sister what happened. She said, "Sometimes he'd listen to me." The other let her try, so away we went again. This time he kind of loosened a little but not enough.

He agreed to take the medicine bundle way out in the woods somewhere and hang it up there.

I told him, "You might as well sleep with it if that is the case, because nowhere in this entire world is too far for those spirits. They go to and fro over the earth. The only way to get rid of them is to burn everything that belongs to them. There is no other way. The Bible says so.[49]

"I know it is a guarantee that the Blood of Jesus will break that curse, yet he won't let go. To think he had one foot in the grave." I told the sisters, "It's no use. It won't work. You see, according to the sisters he received Christ but it wasn't rooted in him. He had no teaching. All of the teaching he ever received was Indian spirituality. Until now he didn't know it wasn't from God. I think he got a shock and then got confused because I was also thought that Indian religion was from God."

Oh, my poor sisters were saddened and hurt because they loved their brother so much. I exhorted them by telling them not to give up. Keep after him. If he finally agrees, burn everything and ask Jesus to break that curse. It will happen. After this disappointing ordeal, the sister brought me to another relative's home – a man and his wife and three children with one being a young adolescent girl. They explained to them who I was. They were very happy to meet me. They asked if I was the one who came to the community fall just this last weekend to hold gospel meetings.

I said, "No, I just got here today."

They both needed prayer for some unknown reason they didn't go to those meetings, although they knew about the meetings.

I spent approximately two hours doing deliverance. When I was done, they told me about their teenage daughter. She seemed to be demon-possessed. We really have to watch for her, especially at nights. "The first time we found

[49] Deut 7:25-26

out I just couldn't get myself to believe what she did. She was walking these roads on the reservation all night long without wearing any clothes or footwear. Mind you, this was mid-winter, and several time they told me we caught her on the road before she got too far. From that time on, we had to take turns watching her all night. One good thing is that she doesn't do this during the day. We tried so hard to lead her to the Lord but she just wouldn't do it. We begged her so many times."

I asked, "Where is she?" "She is in her bedroom."

I also asked them, "Does she understand when you talk to her?" "Yes," they said. "There is nothing wrong in that area. She can communicate." I said, "Is it all right if I talk with her?" They said, "By all means." They told me what room she was in, so I knocked on her door, and I heard her say, "Come in."

I walked in and there was this beautiful young girl. She was tall and slender, and she was lying on her stomach with her feet up above her thighs. She was fooling around with her fingernails.

I introduced myself and shook her hand, and I told her about what I do and why I was on that reservation – that I come to pray for people that need prayer. I asked her if I could sit, and she said, "Yes."

I know that she hadn't accepted Christ but just to get a conversation going, I asked her if she knew Jesus as her personal Savior and she said, "No." I followed up and asked if she would like to know Him but she said, "My parents have been trying to force me to accept but I don't want to."

I told her, "But you do know why your parents are doing that, don't you? It's because they love you very much. They are trying to help you."

I started ministering to her about the Word of God, that God also loves her, that God sacrificed Jesus, God's only begotten Son to be nailed to the cross just for her, and the only way you can get set free is through the shed blood of Jesus Christ.

Then I told her my testimony of how I got set free. She seemed to be listening very closely to my testimony. After I was through I asked again if she wanted to receive Christ into her life and this time she agreed. I led her through the sinner's prayer. When we came to "I believe Jesus died for me", it seemed she started to choke every time she tried to say JESUS. She started to move around and got very jumpy. Her parents came in trying to help her to settle down.

After trying many times she finally managed to say JESUS. When we completed the sinner's prayer, then the battle started. That demon just refused to come out. It screamed out profanity on and on and she fought us. I don't exactly remember how long we wrestled with that demon before it let go. Finally she started vomiting, after that saliva, and at the same time she was crying. It seemed her human self got frightened. I don't think she grasped what was happening to her. When it was all over, I got to explain to her what just took place. Four people got set free and one we lost although he had Christ. I wished he would have gotten delivered and healed. All in all, the trip there wasn't at all lost.

SHORT STORIES

I was taught to be afraid of storms starting at a very young age. My parents and relatives talked of the devastations a storm can leave behind and the things it could destroy in its path. My mother told me this story about a fierce storm that came through when she was just a child. The thing that was so amazing in this story was the presence of the evil that came with this storm. She said there were indescribable sounds mixed in with this storm that frightened her to a point where her body jerked and bounced inches off her bed when she was dozing off to sleep. She suffered from loss of sleep and exhaustion caused from her fear after this storm.

She had been in a lot of storms since that experience, but she never heard the same sounds she heard then. These sounds she heard were from an animal, and no storm sounds like that. She used to say "I am positively without a doubt sure that there was an evil spirit with that storm. There was this clattering sound like a motor with a bad knock would make. The "cluck, cluck, cluck", a growling noise like a lion would not make that roar, that throaty kind of purring. Then this awful blowing exactly like a bull elk would make during rutting season with the bugle. The other thing was it was amplified to an extent that it drowned out the thunder."

She used to mention about this little dog she used to have. "That little dog was also terrified to horror. The fur on the back of this dog's neck was standing straight out, and as frightened as the little dog was, it still tried to defend me. It was on its hind legs most of the time while barking with everything it had, which sounded like yelping." To top it all off, she was home alone with her grandmother who was just a petite, little woman. They were out on their hunting grounds with no one else around. Her uncle was out on foot somewhere probably caught in that same storm hunting for game. They were living in a tent among huge trees. "I thought if the storm didn't kill us a big fallen tree would. The wind was vicious. I am sure a tornado touched down somewhere near where we were camped," she used to say. She used to tell me that her aunty took out her medicine bundle and unraveled her little kind of greenish-colored peace pipe. She started burning incense, making a peace pipe presentation and started talking to that evil spirit to leave them alone. She talked to it in a scolding sense, like a rebuke.

Her aunty said to this spirit, "Who do you think you are, coming here scaring my child like this? We don't want you here, so just go away and leave us alone, and don't do us no harm!" With that she said she finished smoking her peace pipe, and not too long afterward the storm subsided. She used to tell me, it is believed by the Indian people that when you've been frightened in this manner, the way she was terrified, that the spirit in that human will leave. So when that jerking and bouncing continued days after the storm, her aunty went outside and started calling me back facing a different direction each time she called, calling for my spirit to return into my body. She told me so many stories of the perilous times and also funny good times.

Trail Ride

I was invited to preach at the Ranchman's Inn sponsored by the Cowboy Church in Calgary, Alberta. Before the service a White sister in Christ approached me for prayer. When I was done praying for her, she said, "I would have liked my husband to get prayer, too, but he doesn't think he needs it, although I know he does. He had come into contact with the Indian religion but he doesn't think there is anything wrong with getting involved. It's no big deal to him."

So when the service was all over that same sister brought her husband (who was also White) to me. It was then that her husband told me why his wife thinks that he should get prayer. He said that they have a small ranch somewhere south of Calgary where they raise horses. Many times throughout the summer months they go trail riding. During this trail ride they happened to enter an Indian reservation land but in order to continue their trail ride, they had to get permission from whoever lived on that area of reserve land. It happened that an old Indian man lived there. They went to him to ask if they could go across and back through his property.

The old Indian man said, "Yes, of course, you could. But only after you agree to have a peace pipe ceremony with me each time you go through."

What they were actually expecting was a financial payment, but a peace pipe ceremony? 'Heck, no problem.' So they made an agreement. They all got down off their horses and went inside the old Indian man's house where they were going to hold the peace pipe ceremony to seal their agreement.

So, this is what they did each time they entered that part of the Indian reservation. They thought it was a fantastic deal just to smoke a peace pipe. They thought nothing of it.

This was why his wife was getting after him to get prayer. He told me the same thing he told his wife. "There is nothing wrong with it."

Anyway, I told him, "Well if you think there is nothing wrong, why don't you get prayer to prove her wrong? We can do it right here and now if you will let me."

His wife was standing right there listening. He said, "Okay, let's do it."

So I started by making him renounce that agreement he had with the old Indian man. After that I asked the LORD to break the soul ties he made with the old man. Then I came against the ancestral spirits that transferred by way of the peace pipe ceremony. I asked the spirit guides and medicines to release and let go of the stronghold it had on the brother.

All of a sudden the brother started staggering around trying to grab tables and chairs. Instead he was knocking them over whichever way he staggered. Then he started gagging and coughing. Saliva came out of his mouth unto the floor. Then it was all over as suddenly as it started. He was set free. He sat down, and he couldn't even find the words to say. He was just shaking his head.

Finally, he said, "How could something so harmless pack such a hard, evil punch?" I had to explain how all of this came about. I told him when you agreed to the old Indian man's proposal to have a peace pipe ceremony, you submitted yourself and surrendered yourself to his ways and beliefs of the spirit world. You opened a channel for those spirits to enter.

What makes it so easy is because you see it as just a harmless gesture, not realizing how subtle and sly the devil is. The brother didn't even know he was possessed. His wife was the only one who detected that her husband had contracted ancestral spirits from having contact with witchcraft through the Indian religion.

You always have to be on guard. You can't let your guard down for a minute, or else you'll step into the enemy's trap. The peace pipe is considered to have a lot of power. It's held in high regard as sacred. Anyone carrying the peace pipe is considered to have spiritual powers. Not just anyone is allowed.

I know some refuse to carry the peace pipe because of the dangers of mishandling or defiling it. The repercussions are too serious and severe. Even if you misplace it inadvertently, you are not forgiven. So you have to guard it with your life. It's not something you play with.

Something that I read from a testimony in a book long ago suddenly came back to me. This is about sanctifying items. This one brother kept his habit of smoking after he became a Christian. One day he was confronted by this brother who wrote the book that the habit of smoking is a stumbling block to others, and that he should quit.

The answer he got back was like what these Indian brothers who claim that you can redeem articles used in religious beliefs by sanctifying them and to re-use them in the gospel of Jesus Christ.

He said, "I pray and sanctify the cigarette before I smoke it, so there's nothing wrong in smoking. If you find something to contradict what I did and prove that it is wrong, then I'll quit smoking."

The brother told him, "Come over to my place tomorrow and I'll prove it to you." But the brother didn't have the faintest idea what or why he said that. He thought about it all night long. "What am I going to do when he comes?"

The next day this brother came, and he said, "Show me." The brother heard the Spirit of God say, "Take him outside." He told the other brother, "Come outside and I'll show you."

When they got outside, this brother still didn't know why the Spirit of God told him to go outside. Then he heard the Spirit of God say, "Keep walking," so they slowly walked. Again he heard the Spirit of God say, "Stop." He stopped.

This brother again heard the Spirit of God say, "Look down." He looked down and there at his feet were dog feces. He heard God's Spirit say, "Tell him to pick it up, then pray on it and sanctify it, and then eat it."

The moral of this story is that all the sanctifying and redeeming things from the world is not of God.

YOU CAN'T HELP GOD (TO IMPROVE HIS PLAN)

God's Word the Bible is the final authority, the ultimate teaching on how man should live, high above governments and their laws. Man's ways don't even come near what God the Father has put together in the Bible. The Scripture says,

> *"as for God, His way is perfect."*[50]

And yet, as men and women (humans) we still think we can help God with our own thoughts and our own ideas, even though the Word of God warns us of that in Isaiah

> *"For My thoughts are not your thoughts, neither are your ways My ways, For as the heavens are higher than the earth, so are My ways higher than your ways, and My thoughts than your thoughts."*[51]

In my twenty-one years since the Lord Jesus found me, I witnessed so many of my brothers and sisters try their hand in helping God. I have seen brothers and sisters (who were already married to a Christian and vice versa) search for a right partner that they think is perfect for their lives or their ministry. Some of the brothers were married to perfectly good Christian wives, but they thought their wives were not

---

[50] Psalms 18:30

[51] Isaiah 55:8-9

good enough for their ministry. They found different wives fit for their ministry.

It never works that way, for God will never contradict His Word.

> *"let God be true but every man a liar."*[52]

Also,

> *"He saith I know him and keepeth not his commandment is a liar, and the truth is not in him."*[53]

As long as I can remember our family, the Kootenays, loved singing. Like I said in my first book, I could not play a guitar but I could sing. I used to compete in talent shows where they had backup music and finally when the Lord Jesus found me, saved me and healed me, I started going to every gospel meeting that I heard of. There for the first time I saw brothers and sisters sing together with their husbands and wives. Did they ever sound beautiful!

I never thought of this in all the time I sang in the world, but, all of a sudden I wished that my late wife should have had a singing voice so that we could sing together and that could have put the final touches on the ministry that God had given us. You see, my late wife couldn't carry a tune if her life depended on it.

I used to be envious of my brothers in the Lord who had a wife that had a voice and could sing. The enemy used to constantly taunt me with it, to a point where I was thinking maybe I should look around, kind of scout around, for another woman that has a voice and that can sing.

I found out real fast how easy it was to fall into temptation. Like I said in the first book, I did a lot of singing even before I came to Christ, although I couldn't play an

[52] Romans 3:4

[53] 1 John 2:4

instrument until after I came to Christ. I enjoyed singing, so every gospel meeting or gospel jamboree I got all excited to sing. It was during those times I watched my brothers in Christ singing with their wives. Oh my, did they ever sound beautiful!

I used to sing alone because my late wife couldn't carry a note, and I got frustrated wishing and envying my brothers on how blessed they were. At times I wish I had a wife that could sing.

Maybe the ministry God gave me would excel then. Slowly the enemy started putting thoughts in my head. I wanted to drum up some kind of excuse to divorce my wife and find one who could sing. That would be helping God. I thought, 'This would probably bring in more souls for God.' I felt justified, because it's part of the gospel. Although it's not part of the gospel but that's based on what I saw practiced.

> *"There is a way which seemeth right unto man,*
> *But the end thereof are the ways of death."*[54]

Also in John:

> *Go sin no more lest a worst thing come upon thee."*[55]

In Hebrews:

> *"It is a fearful thing to fall into the hands of the living God."*[56]

So when the devil infiltrates unawares into a born again Christian's life by way of disobedience, they wouldn't even know it happened. Let this be a warning. Make sure you

[54] Proverbs 14:12
[55] John 5:14
[56] Hebrews 10:31

double-check your walk. You may be walking and working outside of God's will. False miracles can still happen to keep you blinded, because we as born again Christians are warring against a very crafty and subtle enemy.

> *"For false christs and false prophets shall rise, and shall shew signs and wonders to seduce, if it were possible, even the elect."*[57]

Jesus warns us:

> *"But take heed; behold, I have foretold you all things."*[58]

You have to be totally sold out for Jesus and stand on His Word. Don't waver. That's the only way to defeat the devil. For those of you that have been caught in this snare, please, I beg you, repent from your disobedience, make it right with God while there is still time. Let go of your false pride and humble yourselves. It is not worth it to die in your sin. Let the Word of the Almighty overcome your mindset.

Jesus said,

> *"If your right eye offends you, pluck it out. If your right hand offends you cut it off"*[59]

Meaning, it is better to go to Heaven with one eye than to go to hell with both eyes, and the same with your right arm. Even if you are highly regarded in Christian ministry, it is better to lose it and go to Heaven than to keep it because of hidden sin and end up in hell.

Okay, let's try this one. To a wife or a husband that had been married to a Christian – you're the only one that knows in your heart, no one knows except God, that you

---

[57] Mark 13:22

[58] Mark 13:23

[59] Matthew 18:9

have taken a second wife or a second husband in sin. You have left your Christian spouse on a trumped-up charge, just for the lust of the flesh or to better your ministry. Maybe the lust of the eye, just to look good on stage and to people around you, and you've gone too far and too deep in this relationship. It has grown to be a stronghold in your life. You have been around the Christian circles for many years already with this wife or husband. Do you think you could abandon this relationship for Jesus? This could also go with a common law relationship to a married wife or husband.

The Scripture from Matthew could fit right here:

> *"He that loveth father or mother more than Me is not worthy of me; and he that loveth son or daughter more than me is not worthy of Me."*[60]

This could go the same with husband/wife or common law husband/wife. I give all of the credit to God Almighty. It took a while, but I found out before the devil wrapped his evil hands around my neck that singing only had a small part of the ministry that God has given me. We should all know by now that the devil doesn't just give up like us humans do. If he doesn't get you one way he'll try another, and another, and another. There is a saying, "I'll die trying." Well, we'll die, while he's trying, if we are strong in God's Word. The Word of God says,

> *"For those that endure to the end them shall be saved."*[61]

The devil is a conspirator. He'll even help you kill yourself. That's precisely what he's trying to set up in your life. He'll make you conspire against God's Word, by all

---

[60] Matthew 10:37
[61] Matthew 24:13

means. Either way he'll try to get you, now or later. He is a very subtle and crafty enemy.

Do you remember when someone cheated you and got the best of you and you realized he'd done this after it was all over? You said, "Boy! Did that person ever take me for a ride!" Well, if we don't watch every step we take, that is exactly what the devil will do to you. All the while you thought, "What a deal!" or "What a steal!" only to find out that the devil had taken you for a long ride. Let's pray that we find the strength to get off before this ride is over, or that we don't get on at all.

I would say to myself, "And if you find such a woman, then what?" Once the devil got me thinking his way, he threw ideas in my mind, 'Get a divorce.' "How?" I would say to myself, "On what grounds?" 'Scheme some kind of evil device to cause a divorce,' he would say.

In times like these I thought it would be justifiable. After all, I was only trying to help God to better the ministry He had given me. The Word of God says in Proverbs,

> *"There is a way which seemeth right unto a man,*
> *But the end thereof are the ways of death."*[62]

Also in Mark it says,

> *"What therefore God hath joined together, let not man put asunder. And in the house his disciples asked him again of the same matter. And he saith unto them, 'Whosoever shall put away his wife, and marry another, committeth adultery against her. And if a woman shall put away her husband, and be married to another, she committeth adultery.'"*[63]

[62] Proverbs 14:12
[63] Mark 10:9-12

The devil made sure that the Word of God never interfered with my sinful thoughts. He kept me away from searching the Scriptures, if what I am thinking of doing was right. To make matters worse, I started bumping into Christian brothers and sisters who had done just that and it seemed like their ministry never slackened.

I never shared this with anyone. I kept those thoughts to myself. My late wife never knew the wicked, evil thoughts that the enemy had planted in my head. When a person follows up and does these evil plans, that person allowed the enemy (the devil) to infiltrate into the ministry that God had given them. Suddenly that person's ministry is turned over to the enemy. God's ministry is replaced by the angel of light. It's so subtle; the devil just slides himself in.

> *"The devil as a roaring lion walketh about, seeking whom he may devour,"*[64]

so the enemy is always watching for a chance to snare a disobedient child. The Bible states,

> *"Blessed are they that do His commandments that they may have right to the tree of life, and may enter in through the gates into the city."*[65]

So you might say, "How is it that miracles and signs and wonders still happen after Christians knowingly and deliberately break God's commandments?" Always remember the devil can imitate God, and don't forget the Scripture:

> *"And the devil said to Him (Jesus), 'all this power will I give thee, and the glory of them; for that is*

---

[64] 1 Peter 5:8

[65] Revelation 22:14

delivered unto me, and to whomsoever I will I give it.' "[66]

So if you are looking for signs and wonders, the devil surely can do that. The devil stole this power from Adam and he will continue having this power until his end comes.

Remember he (devil) can quote Scriptures and use them. In Luke 4:10 he paraphrased what Jesus kept saying,

> *"For it is written", And the devil also said 'For it is written, He shall give His angels charge over Thee, to keep Thee, And in their hands they shall bear Thee up, lest at any time Thou dash Thy foot against a stone.'*[67]

and he quoted this Scripture from Psalm 91:11-12.

When a disobedient Christian has allowed this religious spirit into his ministry and another Christian can be fooled because this minister (the disobedient one) will sound just like a genuine, straight-and-narrow Christian. He is using the same Scriptures and doing what a straight-and-the-narrow walking Christian does, all except his fruits are not the same.

In 2 Corinthians, it says,

> *"And no marvel, for satan himself is transformed into an angel of light, Therefore it is no great thing if his ministers also be transformed as the ministers of righteousness, whose end shall be according to their works."*[68]

Remember the Scripture in Matthew:

---

[66] Luke 4:6

[67] Luke 4:10-11

[68] 2 Corinthians 11:14-15

> *"Not everyone that saith unto Me, 'Lord, Lord', shall enter into the kingdom of heaven; but he that doeth the will of my Father which is in heaven. Many will say to me in that day, 'Lord, Lord, have we not prophesied in Thy name? And in Thy name have cast out devils and in Thy name done many wonderful works?' And then will I profess unto them, I never knew you; depart from Me, ye that work iniquity."*[69]

Remember in Matthew

> *"And if Satan cast out Satan, he is divided against himself; how shall then his kingdom stand?"*[70]

But once again, the devil tried another angle approximately a year after my first wife went home to be with Jesus. I ran into some turbulence, caused by my own fault. I am a too-trusting person when it comes to Christianity. I naturally think Christians are all the same, meaning sold out for Jesus. I didn't realize that there are many supposedly Christians out there that use Christians for their own needs (non-Christians also).

We born-again Christians are very vulnerable because of the teaching from the Scriptures – to be kind, helpful, sharing, etc. Supposedly Christians and non-Christians alike tend to use this opportunity of openness to their advantage. My wife Mary Ann told me stories about non-Christian men who would purposely go to Christian activities such as church picnics and suppers just to pounce on women. She even said some went as far as going to the altar to snare a born-again Christian woman and proclaim they were Christians. The Bible calls these "*wolves in sheep's clothing*".

---

[69] Matthew 7:21-23

[70] Matthew 12:26

Anyway, after my wife of thirty-five years died, I continued ministering. Although I cried half of the time with heartbreak and sorrow, I stayed on the road. Every place I went was a reminder of our travels but I couldn't just isolate myself in a room, so I tried to alleviate my pain by getting out and doing something. I also got so much comfort to be around a gospel meeting with my Christian brothers and sisters.

After five or six months the Lord finally made me realize that my wife was home in Glory with Jesus. There ain't no two ways about her death – I just had to accept it. It was then the Lord gave me peace and took away all the pain. Although at times I missed her companionship, the pain wasn't there anymore. Sometimes when I was far away from home on some dark, lonely highway by myself, it would cross my mind when I wished I had someone to talk to, someone to share my feelings with. I would wonder maybe someday if I lived long enough that I might meet that special someone.

Other than that, my focus was strictly on the gospel. If it ever happened, I would want God to pick and choose the one just for me. One thing I knew for sure was the person has to be free to travel, love Jesus, and love to evangelize full time, because that's what I did. Another thing was that the person had to be around my age – a few years older or a few years younger.

Another time before I realized that singing only played a small part, I again almost fell into a trap. This happened right after I lost my first wife, after she had gone home to be with Jesus. Approximately a year later I met a sister in Christ, which eventually led me to meet her younger sister who needed deliverance. I thought she was just perfect for the ministry that God had given me, and she called a meeting together at her place where I was invited to speak on the bondage of Indian religion. They cooked a big lunch, and we spoke while we sat around the table.

Afterward they disclosed their struggle with curses spoken unto their family tree. I then did some deliverance to most of them, a couple of them didn't have time and they had to leave, but the rest got set free. It wasn't long afterward this younger sister called, so I went back to her place. She had so much more garbage. She needed cleaning, not only in her life but also her place. To make a long story short, things went well for her and a year went by. Again, I overlooked certain facts in this sister's life that almost caused me to fall fully into the hands of the devil.

I got to know her pretty well. She was divorced once to her man of twenty some odd years before she met Christ, but she still had a close contact with him. Actually she told me that her first husband spent some nights at her place, which never bothered me, because we were just friends.

She told me that she was separated from her husband for three and a half years, and that she was seeking a divorce. She tried very hard to divorce her second husband whom she said was not a Christian, and that she had a right to divorce him. Her second husband wouldn't release her. She even went as far as serving him with divorce papers and he wouldn't take it. There could never be a reconciliation with him ever. I just thought she needed to get this off her chest.

Oh, I tell you, she knew the Word and she was also into deliverance. To top it all off, she had a unique singing voice. Although she couldn't sing, with some help she could turn out to be a fantastic singer. Just what I, not God, was looking for. She also had no children, nothing to tie her down. For two years we tried in vain for her divorce.

Right after that younger sister's deliverance, I noticed that she had a very unique singing voice. With a little help, she could turn out to be a fantastic singer. From that time on, I tried my hand at teaching her what I knew about singing, and I helped her record a CD including a song that I wrote called, "I Finally Met My Man", meaning Jesus was "the man". One day after a year and a half, I made her record that song in a studio with just an acoustic guitar, and could follow the beat and keep time.

In all that time we stayed away from fornicating or sleeping together, but I got very attached to her. She also took time off work to follow me with her friends to evangelize wherever I was called. They saw firsthand how the Holy Spirit moved in those services.

One time I stopped at my dear sister in Christ that always supported my ministry to pick up some tithes that she had for me. It was then she first met this younger sister. It happened that she and her friend and my daughter were going with me to minister in B.C. (British Columbia), which was a fair piece of traveling.

I had been warned about this sister that I was involved with by a couple of elderly Christian sisters who are totally sold out to Jesus, quoting the same Scriptures that I used in this short story about divorce. They kept telling me that this sister not only made a lifetime promise to her husband when she got married, but also made a covenant with God that she is not supposed to break. I had tunnel vision and I listened to the lies of this sister that her husband was never a Christian and by this she had a right to divorce him. I found out a long time later that this man attended church every Sunday and he played music for the church.

She also used Scripture to back up her intent.

> *"For the unbelieving husband is sanctified by the wife and the unbelieving wife is sanctified by her husband; else were your children unclean: but now are they holy. But if the unbelieving depart, let him depart. A brother or a sister is not under bondage in such cases: but God hath called us to peace."*[71]

---

[71] 1 Corinthians 7:14, 15

These Scriptures were not from the Lord according to Paul in verse 12. Paul says, "But to the rest speak I, not the Lord." She also used the Scripture,

> *"do not be unequally yoked with unbelievers, turn away from such."*

The next time my dear sister brought down some new converts down to my house for baptismal, I told this younger sister what I was going to do on Sunday. She arrived to help. She came face to face with my dear sister again who is an old Christian warrior, and she doesn't miss much, and she is always aware of things. Usually she is quiet and doesn't say much, but when she talks, she speaks with authority, and I listen.

My dear sister in Christ used these exact words, "Who was that woman who came with you when you were at my house? My dear sister asked me, "Why is that woman following you around?" I told her that she says she is only my friend, and she would like to help me minister whenever possible.

I told her all about her – the counselling, the teaching, deliverance, etc. – everything. After I finished, she looked me square in the eye and said, "You watch yourself with that woman. She's up to no good."

Once again, my dear sister gave me that look, and she said, "She lies. She is after you. You watch her, and she'll show herself." My dear sister has a gift of discernment. I know that for a fact. For almost two years of knowing this younger sister, there was no indication of ever suspecting that she intended to have me for a husband, never, and I believed her because she never even so much as hinted that she had an interest in me other than being a friend.

If this younger sister was after me, why didn't she make her move a long time ago? What is she waiting for? Then I thought about her divorce. Maybe that's what she's got in mind of doing after she divorces her husband but she's not telling me. All sorts of *maybe's* went through my mind. But when I left Alberta she was back with her husband, so there is the answer. She wasn't after me after all.

Usually I can spot a setup a mile away, if she was setting me up. Then I would say she was more subtle than the devil himself because everything she said and did so far was genuine, at least in what I picked up from her so far. Now, when my dear sister said those things, it sent shock waves through my poor mind. I was like an umpire in a baseball game trying to make a call at home plate where the runner slide home – was he safe or was he out? And I didn't make the call right away instead I kind of rolled it around in mind first putting my head side to side. Without making a call, I felt like throwing my mask down and throwing my indicator as far as I could into the crowd and walk away. I started getting paranoid.

I feel so blessed today that her divorce never came through. Her husband who professed to be a Christian stood his ground on the Word of God, and he would not release her. Otherwise I'd be one of those brothers or sisters that are convinced they are justified and are helping God. I would have been committing adultery if she would have gotten her divorce and I married her. That's according to the Word of God,

> *"And if a woman shall put away her husband, and be married to another, she committeth adultery."*[72]

I was still close to her even though I was out ministering many times during the time this was happening. One time we had a verbal disagreement over supper. I thought, 'Well, if she's not going to listen, no use wasting my time.' and I left.

---

[72] Mark 10:12

About a week later she called me and wanted to see me, so I went. She apologized and we started talking again. It was then that she confessed of spending a night with her first husband again, committing adultery. When this happened, I saw her weakness was still controlling her life. I said to myself, 'No wonder she's not getting along with her husband.'

I sat there in awe listening to what happened. All the while she was crying in between sobs of regret. She promised the Lord and me as a witness that it will never happen again. All of the fasting and praying helped, because I witnessed the change from the time I first met her until then.

I felt betrayed and let down. I thought the Lord and I accomplished something good here but now I didn't even know how to react. It took several days to swallow down what I experienced. It eventually subsided and I left to go north. I spent about a week there.

When I got home, I got a call that there was a big conference happening in Saskatchewan, and I decided to go. I only spent overnight at home when I got a call from her. She told me that she was back with her husband, and I was honestly happy for her. I left for Regina, Saskatchewan, to the conference. There I met some brothers from the Standing Buffalo Reservation who were Dakota Sioux, and that is where I stayed for the winter ministering around the area.

I also met someone at the conference who played a big part in meeting my present wife Mary Ann. This sister, who was from the Turtle Mountain Indian Reservation (the Chippewa Band), lived in Bismarck, North Dakota, and she kept in contact with me by phone. When a group of Christians and a couple of ministers were going to South Dakota, they asked me to join them. I naturally went along. There I met a brother who invited me back to minister in a place called White River, South Dakota. It was then that I made first contact with Mary Ann.

It was the time I was coming back to Canada when I stopped at Bismarck to spend the night. I called my contact. The next morning I got a call in my room, and the sister suggested breakfast at KFC. I said, "Okay, we'll do that after I clean up." I packed my belongings and checked out.

I headed straight for KFC where I met the sister with her future son-in-law. It was then over breakfast that she phoned Mary Ann, who was sick and didn't go to work that day. After she talked with Mary Ann, she handed me her cell phone and said, "Talk to her." I wasn't expecting this, but still I took her offer.

For the first time I spoke with my future wife, and of course, I didn't know this at the time. She couldn't come out because she was sick, so I had to leave without meeting her face to face. I never knew how she looked; I just knew her voice. I had her phone number that her friend gave to me, so when I was almost at the border, I called her. From that time on we communicated by phone.

When I got back to my brothers in Christ's home where I was staying, I decided to go home and visit my children. When I got home everything was still in order, and nothing had changed. My daughter and her kids were especially happy that I was back. My daughter was attending school studying Business Management, and she lived on the south side of the city of Edmonton. I told her about Mary Ann, and she told me to ask Mary Ann if she had an email address.

I got Mary Ann's email address, and my daughter started talking to her through her computer. I know nothing about computers, as I am what you call computer illiterate, not only computer illiterate. I used to type using one finger at a time when I worked as a substance abuse counsellor.

My daughter sat me down at her computer and told me to look at the screen. "You see words, read them. That's Mary Ann talking, and all you got to do is type in your answer, like this..." She began typing. Mary Ann is a very fast typist. By the time I got one word edgewise, it would disappear off the screen, but I sat there punching in words the best I could. After we finished typing, she asked me to pray, so I typed in a prayer.

Now it had been a long time ago since I left Alberta and I never had contact with the younger sister since then. I more or less forgot about her until she called me at home. She told me that she was running into problems with her husband to a point that they hadn't even been sleeping together. I thought, 'Oh, well, they'll iron it out somehow. It's not my problem.'

Anyway I got a phone call from Regina that a pastor wanted to talk to me. I phoned the pastor and he said, "We are setting up some meetings in a couple of weeks, and we want you to come and minister. Will you be free?"

"Of course I'm free. I am just here visiting my children."

"So be it," he said. "We'll be expecting you."

A lot of things took place in between those two weeks. I got a phone call from the younger sister and asked if I could meet her at the west end Wal-Mart. I went down there and we had lunch together. She said, "I'm kicking out my husband." I said, "What! Are you sure?" She said, "I have to, before I go crazy."

That was it for that. Then she called me on my cell while I was at my daughter's place around supper time, and she told me all about life with her husband.

I told her about my commitment to minister in Regina. This is when I all of a sudden heard what my dear sister warned me about, from out of the slip of the tongue or intentionally. She said, "I should have realized that it would never work and I stayed away from taking him back. I should have known that you were the one to have for a husband." By this time I wanted nothing to do with her. I had been gone too long to care. I think she knew that too, by the way I responded.

A few days later I paid her a visit at her work on my way to Regina. I said my farewells and I left. She later told me that somehow she felt that this was going to be the last time, which it was, because I stayed in Regina and kept on ministering, and all the while I had contact with Mary Ann.

By this Scripture Jesus was saying that the devil is not dividing his kingdom. It only looks like it. I can attest to this Scripture. When I was practicing the Indian religion we would have what we called "medicine wars". Medicine men war against medicine men or medicine women against medicine women. A spiritual battle would take place trying to prove whose power is more superior. At the end one would look like a winner. But none of these medicine men or medicine women was saved. They were all filled with unclean spirits, which means the devil was only playing games. None were winners because they were all in darkness. When the devil infiltrates into a born-again Christian's life by way of disobedience, they wouldn't even know it. SO let this be a warning and double check your walk. You may be walking and working outside of God's will, because we as born-again Christians are fighting against a very subtle enemy. The Word of God states,

> *"If it were possible he will fool the very elect. For false christs and false prophets shall rise. And shall shew signs and wonders, to seduce, if it were possible, even the elect."* [73]

In Mark Jesus warns us,

> *"But take ye heed: behold, I have foretold you all things."*[74]

[73] Mark 13:22

[74] Mark 13:23

While you still have time to repent, please, I beg you, turn from your disobedience and make it right with God. Let go of your false pride and humble yourselves. It's not worth it to die in your sin. Let the Word of the Almighty overcome your mindset. I am so glad that I did not fall in the trap of the devil, because I found out singing wasn't my ministry. Deliverance is what the Lord had given me. It was because I loved singing that the devil tried to deceive me to disobey God. I still like to sing but I do not use it to an extent to sidetrack me.

One day a miracle took place. God healed a young medicine man in my ministry that God had given me, and a great fire lit up. A revival started, and it was during those revivals on the big meeting we had at an old school gym.

I phoned Mary Ann and I asked her if it was possible for her to come to Canada to this revival. I told her all what happened, and she came. For the first time after speaking to her on the phone, I was going to see her face to face. I was all excited. I could hardly contain myself. Just hours before the meeting started, she called me from a little town called Qu'Appelle while I was waiting for her in Ft. Qu'Appelle. I used to think that she also was going to see me for the first time, but she later told me she read the first book and she saw a picture of me on the back cover.

After the weekend revival was all over, it was time for her to go. I offered her lunch. I don't remember the exact time that I threw out the Big Question, if it was before lunch or after. I thought, 'It's now or never.'

I said, "What would you say if I asked you to marry me?" She said yes, so I decided to travel back with her to Bismarck, North Dakota, where we got married ten days later.

Several of my brothers and sisters really felt that I did the wrong thing by marrying a White sister in the Lord. They were convinced because the ministry God had given me involved Indian religion, and that my calling was for the

Indian people of Canada and the United States. It's only fitting that my wife be a Christian Indian woman also.

Looking back at the way it happened, the devil used even the ministers of the gospel to try to defuse our marriage. There were some very prominent ministers who approached me on this matter that almost caused a separation in my marriage right off the bat. Instead of going to God seeking for an answer, I went to seek advice from man, which was a mistake. I should have been on my face before God crying for His will, although God still prevailed.

I almost divorced my wife within one month of our marriage because of this discouragement. To think I would have not gotten married again, just so long as one of us was still alive.

> *"For the woman which hath an husband is bound by the Law to her husband so long as he liveth; but if the husband be dead, she is loosed from the law of her husband. So then, if, while her husband liveth, she be married to another man, she shall be called an adulterer: but if her husband be dead, she is free from that Law; so that she is no adulterer, though she be married to another man."*[75]

When I thought of it, the Word of God is the Word of God, no matter who it comes out from: Red, White, Black or Yellow.

To me, I had no hope left. I totally gave up on our marriage. I was completely defeated. I said, "What in the world is going on? Why is this happening to me?" First I lost my first wife and along with that, I almost lost my mind from pain, heartbreak and sorrow. Then, my plans with the sister in the Lord I met didn't work out. Now I met this beautiful White sister in the Lord and I married her.

---

[75] Romans 7:2, 3

Most of my so-called Christian friends thought it was all wrong. Trouble was I listened to them, which caused all of the confusion.

I was at my daughter's place racking my brains and pacing the floor, talking to myself. I remember even cursing myself for being so stupid. When I said, "I guess I was meant to be alone," this was going to take everything out of me. I was married to my first wife for thirty-five years and that is very rare nowadays. To think that I was going to join the "Get Married and Break Up Right Away Club" in my old age just didn't sit right with me. "But, so be it, OK!" I said to myself," "I made my mind up that I am never going to reconcile with my wife. I decided to go it alone, never ever again I'm ever going to fall for another women, that is it."

Within a short time, I went to a baptismal service in Lebret, Saskatchewan, and I had notified one of the pastors and brothers in the Lord in Regina that I was coming. Meanwhile my wife Mary Ann was asking for prayer from this same pastor in Regina, Saskatchewan. The pastor told her that he plans to talk to me about honoring our marriage vows, and as a man of God, that I need to reconcile with my wife.

At the baptismal service the pastor told me to wait around after the service, because he wanted to talk to me. I asked one of the Christian brothers from their church what the pastor wants to talk to me about. They told me that it has to do with my responsibility for my marriage. I headed home without talking to the pastor, because I didn't see any reason to talk to him. I thought my marriage was over. After all, it was a mistake in the first place. I just wanted to get the divorce and go on with my life, to go alone in the ministry and to forget about women.

A few days later I called my wife Mary Ann and I told her, "You might as well go on with the divorce. I am going on alone to minister the gospel." My voice was cold and I was very defensive. I never asked how she was feeling or what she's been doing.

She said, "The ministers in Regina will not let you minister in their churches because you are not obeying the Word of God. You have turned your back on your marriage and you are not fit to minister. Your ministry is over."

When she said this, I was very defensive and I repeated, "Well, I am going on alone." I hung up the phone.

After this phone call, my wife Mary Ann thought she would never hear from me again, and it devastated her totally. She didn't know what to do, except begin heavy spiritual warfare, claiming her husband that was rightfully hers.

A few weeks later my wife Mary Ann was pounding the floor with her fists crying to God, and God acted on her cries. At the same time when I was at my daughter's apartment, I was on my way to the washroom upstairs because that was the only washroom. Halfway up the flight of stairs something hit me. It seemed like all of this weight of confusion and despair lifted. My whole heart just changed in an instant. Just then I heard this still, small voice say to me, "Repent and humble yourself. Ask Mary Ann for forgiveness."

I felt such a peace about what was impressed in my heart. Mary Ann was home in her apartment in Bismarck, North Dakota, and I was in Edmonton, Alberta, Canada when this happened. I don't even remember making my way back downstairs. I was in such a delightful feeling with glee. The only phone was downstairs, so I picked it up.

That's when the devil used everything to discourage me happened. The devil did his best to control my mind. He tried to stop me from dialing that phone number. He said, "What you heard is not real. She is never going to forgive you. Don't even try. Give it up."

Anyway, with my heart almost coming through my chest, I started dialing. Doubt tried to enter in. 'What are you going to say to her, anyway, if she answers the phone.

What if she is not home? Are you going to have the same strength to try again?'

Then I heard her phone ringing. By then my heart was about to explode with the unknown. Then came the answer of her sweet, loveable voice. I didn't know just how much I missed her until then. I was all choked up when I managed to say "Hello, how are you?". Then I said something that I don't even remember, which broke the extreme tension in my chest and throat and I immediately followed up with what I had in mind of saying before anything else happens.

"Could you forgive me, please? This is your husband Adolph."

It was only then that I found out the devil was bluffing because I heard my wife Mary Ann say, "I forgive you."

Wow! What a feeling! A rush of joy overcame my whole body but even then I tried to keep my composure from sounding too excited. That weekend she came to Edmonton, driving all the way from Bismarck, North Dakota. Although she went back alone, we reconciled. I had committed myself to minister the following weekend; once that was fulfilled, I was free to go back to the States to my Mary Ann, and it happened just that way.

I found out that my wife Mary Ann went to God for her answers, which to me made the difference. Plus, a couple of ministers who never give up interceded for her that our marriage would not break up.

I am happy that I met my second wife Mary Ann. Although she doesn't sing country gospel, she has helped me put this book in the way that God and I want people to understand. It was God who put us together.

Plus, I found out after my wife and I reconciled that she had been working among the Indians (the host people of this country) for sixteen years and grew up with Indian friends and knew a lot of their ways. It really confirmed a lot of things she wondered about when she heard my testimony and started helping me in finishing the book

"Out of Bondage" now that we know each other. It was God, looking back at the way it happened.

From that time on we lived in Bismarck until Mary Ann resigned from her job in May 2004. She had quit her job of sixteen years just before she could receive her pension and she moved to Canada with me to go into full time ministry, something that she always prayed for – the ministry. She had one year until she would receive retirement pension, but it was then that she told me that she was now free to minister and serve the Lord, and that nothing could stand in the way of her going into the ministry with me.

Her sisters thought she lost her mind. They couldn't understand why she would do such a thing when she was so close to retirement, and to leave familiar country to go into an unknown frontier. 76

She is also slowly finishing her own book she started years ago, an autobiography of herself. God is really blessing us and many others that we pray for in our ministry. This time it's until death do us part.

She told me later that she grew up in Bismarck, and she thought she would never leave Bismarck and eventually she would die there. The next time I came back to Canada she packed up and left with me, to leave Bismarck, North Dakota, far behind. Never in her wildest dreams did she ever imagine living in Canada. Praise the Lord! Isn't God awesome?

It reminded me of a song that the First Nations people used to sing. It goes like this:

> *"Darling, don't cry when I leave the U.S.A. If you like, I'll take you home when I go back to Canada."*

---

[76] Genesis12:1-3

THE UNEXPLAINED

One time my wife Mary Ann and I were invited to go to minister in Winnipeg, Manitoba, a couple of years back. We were supposed to stay at this sister's home. It was all arranged before time, but as always the enemy never stops interfering. It so happened that this sister got a surprise visit from her daughter who happened to be living outside of Canada, and she took the room that was supposed to be reserved for us.

When this happened, the group of Christians who invited us quickly made other arrangements for us. We ended up staying at a single mother's place that had three children living with her – two boys and a girl. The young girl, who I guess her age might have been around ten to twelve years old, let us have her room. That same day that we got there this single mom's vehicle broke down. We had a brand new Ford Ranger pickup, so my wife and I decided to let her use it while we were ministering there.

Because we didn't know the area of the city, other brothers and sisters in Christ drove us around. Like I mentioned, the enemy was always lurking around causing conflicts and dissension. It seems just our presence can cause all sorts of reactions from the enemy. We were just visitors but this sister, the single mom, acted like we were her prisoners. She got upset constantly and very easily.

My wife and I were happy and excited to be so far away from home, so every opportunity we had to visit sights or enjoy visiting other Christians we did, not knowing when, or if ever, we'd be back here again.

Because of this we came in late for lunch, dinner and supper that our sister had prepared. Oh man, she'd just go totally ballistic on us. She'd be shouting at us why we were late. My wife and I didn't mind if our meal was cold. We would just throw it in the microwave to warm it up. It was no big deal, but to her, she took it like a slap in the face. We never argued back because we didn't understand her. Even today we still don't know what the big deal was.

This one time we had an afternoon service and nothing planned for the evening. When we heard there was a gospel jamboree just outside of the city, we jumped at the chance of taking in this celebration. That night we came in probably way past midnight, happy as could be because we really enjoyed ourselves at the jamboree. But, I tell you, we heard an earful from this sister the next day.

It so happened that the daughter who was visiting her mother (the other sister who originally invited us to stay) left that day, and we were invited to move there the next day. My wife and I were packing and getting ready, and this sister where we were staying was barely containing her anger.

She was throwing things around and banging doors. All the while my wife either did not detect this single mom's anger or didn't care, because she asked me if we were going to have breakfast there before we leave.

I said, "NO! Let's get out fast before she busts loose!"

I don't think my wife knew why, but she did as I did. I grabbed my bags and quickly got out of the house and hurried to where our truck was packed. We did everything in haste. We threw our luggage in the back of the truck as fast as we could but she came running out with her daughter and proceeded to lash out at us.

I know for a fact that the enemy was behind all of it by the way she acted. I mean, she should have heard herself.

She sounded like we were going places without her approval, that we were supposed to get permission first. It made it look like we were uncontrollable children.

The only thing I finally told her was to act her age. What I was actually saying was that you don't have to go through all these antics of jumping up and down and yelling at us. We can sit down and talk this through as grownups. She didn't even understand that.

We said to her,"We did everything we could. We even as much as let you have our vehicle when your broke down."

She just shouted, "Oh, that gas guzzler? I was better off on foot!"

It wasn't getting us anywhere listening to her, so we drove away. She once even came after me because I got married to a White woman. She asked what was wrong with having an Indian woman for a wife.

There was something really wrong in this sister's life. From this time on she was at every service we were invited, but when she had our truck she never showed up in our meetings. She was somewhere else.

In the Sunday afternoon meeting, my wife sat with this sister and asked her what was bothering her, and the sister was in tears. My wife put her arm around the sister and asked the sister if she could pray for her. The sister agreed, and the sister wept and said that she was going through a very hard time. The sister apologized to my wife. You see, the devil uses every kind of method to cause divisions between Christians, no matter where we are.

Anyway, during the same time, this other sister who did street ministry invited us to minister in these churches that served meals to street people. There the place filled up with homeless who were either high on alcohol or drugs. They didn't care less what took place, just so long as they got their lunch. I don't know what this sister was thinking, but she wanted me to minister to them about what the Indian religion was about – all about the spiritual aspects of it.

I disagreed with her. I said that I'll be just wasting my breath because even the sober Indians don't understand when I minister to them. How are these that are high on drugs or alcohol going to benefit? They need a good salvation message which anyone of the half a dozen that were there could do.

She got mad at me. She just couldn't get through her head that abstaining from the Indian religion wasn't going to help this bunch but that abstaining from drugs and alcohol will. From that time on she abandoned us, and she wouldn't even talk to us.

This all took place in the dead of winter. Afterwards a group of Christians rented a conference room at the Hotel Louis Riel for me to minister. It was set to start at 7 pm. That day around 4 pm a huge snowstorm blew in. Around 6 pm there were weather warnings all around the city. We got to the Hotel Louis Riel around 6:30 pm all set for an evening of glorifying the Lord. We entered the hotel lobby and it was almost full of people. It was surprising because it was a huge lobby but we soon found out why everybody was waiting in the lobby.

The huge snowstorm had caused a power outage, so we joined the crowds waiting for the power to come back on. Finally it was getting on nigh to 8 pm, so we asked the manager if we could start our meeting with the backup system. He refused, due to safety reasons. When it looked like we were never going to have our meeting one of the pastors suggested that we open his church for us to meet. We ended up at his church with only a small part of the people that were at the hotel.

In my years of ministering, I have encountered so many different tactics the enemy uses – always a different device to try to discourage me from ministering the truth, like this power outage centered in one building. You would think a whole section like a one-block radius would have this power outage. But, no, I attribute this negative phenomenon to the enemy – the devil himself – on many occasions. I have been challenged by medicine men/women to try to stop the truth, especially if they had been warned ahead of time of my coming.

Like I told medicine men and women, "You don't have the faintest idea what you are dealing with here. You're dealing with the most clever, sly, subtle power known to man, and it has a stronghold on you. It's an evil force that reigns over you."

I try to get it across to them as clear as I can possibly say by putting it in plain English. They hear me out, but only the good Lord knows if it made any impact.

SPIRITUAL CONNECTION

One day in 2005 I just didn't feel right physically. It was so strange. It wasn't a pain or ache in my body. My head felt a little heavy. I'd get up and sit on my bed and that is as far as I would get. It seemed that my mind won't clear up. My body felt the same – no strength – so I'd just flop back in bed and lay there and wait to see if things would get better. To my amazement that feeling just would not leave. My wife Mary Ann was up and around waiting for me to get up, but I just couldn't. We were planning to take a trip to Florida that week. She was sort of packing at the same time and here I am laid up. I stayed in that bed all day. Every now and again my wife would come in to tell me to "get up, get ready, we are going to Florida, remember?" For the life of me I just couldn't get myself going. Something was definitely wrong. I don't remember ever feeling this way in my life. The last I remember was probably that night.

After that, I never remembered a thing. I thought at one time I heard a warble from an emergency vehicle like in a distance.

The day before my wife Mary Ann told me later that I started acting weird. I started pointing in the closet like I was seeing something funny in there. I would laugh out loud. She knew she had to do something to try to help. I guess she said to me that she should call an ambulance for me. When she said it, I really got upset with her so she held off.

The clincher came when I started urinating on myself and on the bed. Then she knew something drastic happened to me. All of this I don't remember. It was a total blank. The next thing I remember is that I was lying on top of a mattress that was on a floor along a partition. My pillow was on top of a person's feet who was sitting with his back against a wall, his legs propped up against his chest. Somehow I knew this person. There was a sort of spiritual connection because I was talking to him and asking him questions.

This room we were in had all kinds of contraptions that a disabled person might have in their room – some intravenous hook-up stands, oxygen tanks with masks and things that can lift up a person who is unable to move around well on their own. I was asking him, "Who does this stuff belong to that's in this room?"

He told me that it belongs to someone else. Just then this little black person walked into the room at the foot of where I was lying. He was no taller than four feet. His hair on his head made him look four foot because it stood straight up, like a little troll with bowed legs. It waddled like a duck when it walked. He was staring right at me. It wouldn't take its eyes off me as it walked by. All the while I was also staring at it. Once in a while it would take a real quick glance at my friend at the head of where I was lying, and then back to me right away. He'd go to the corner of the room and stand there, staring at me. Then it would walk back out. Just when I thought it walked out of my room, it would stick its head back in one more time before it would disappear.

This little black person came and visited my room three times. He did the same thing each time, and every time this happened, my friend would get me up and take me on the other side of this partition where there was this wall-sized sliding glass door, slide it open and take me outside. It looked to me like he was carrying me but I was always ahead of him. He never was beside me or ahead of me, always behind me. He would take me high up on some hill where there was nothing but grass and we would sit there on that hill. I was always talking but I can't remember what the subject was about. Then he would take me back inside again. On the fourth and last time he took me on that hill, I remember glancing over my shoulder to have a look at him.

He was approximately six foot four inches, tall jet black shoulder-length hair and he looked just like a First Nations man. He was tall and lean. His face was almost round and it shone like an apple with a happy look, like he was always smiling. When he brought me back inside, he laid me on a bed instead of the mattress on the floor. There was a transition that took place, like from spiritual to the present. While I was talking to him, we were interrupted by someone else in the room who started asking me questions.

It was a doctor, and he asked me, "Mr. Kootenay, do you know where you are?" This is where I could hear in the spirit and the present at the same time. When the doctor asked me that question, I was just about to tell him, 'Yeah, I'm in a room somewhere in the basement of this building,' when I heard that man I've been with say, "Tell him you are in the hospital."

Without hesitation I said, "I am in the hospital." Then the doctor asked me, "What hospital?" I didn't know anything. Just then I heard that person that was with me say to me, "Tell him you are in the Royal Alex Hospital." I said, "I am in the Royal Alex Hospital." Then the doctor asked me, "What year is it?" I remembered that it was 2005. I said to the doctor with confidence that it was 2005. I didn't know that I had been in a coma right through the New Year.

If that man I was with all this time didn't correct me, I was sure it was still 2005, but again I heard him say "It's 2006". Right then I had to correct myself. I said, "No, it's 2006." Because of it the doctor quit asking me questions. If I didn't come to at that particular time, my wife Mary Ann told me that they were going to hook me to a life support system.

What actually happened to me was that my kidneys shut down. Once I came to, I remember feeling like nothing was wrong with me. A physical therapist visited the following day to help me walk again. She had a harness to harness me up with. She was planning to hold me up while she walked with me to steady me. I started laughing and said, "I don't think I need to be harnessed up. I think I could walk without it. I could even outrun you."

So she dared me. She thought I was just talking, but I got off that bed and took off out the door and down the hall. She started calling me back. She said, "I believe you. Come back!" I would have been discharged the next day which was a Friday, but they found out I had a low blood count. They decided to give me two pints of blood and that caused them to keep me through the weekend. I was discharged on Monday. That weekend we left for Florida.

NOT THE SAME REVERENCE

I always wanted to mention a huge concern that hits me. When I am out ministering for the Gospel of Jesus Christ, I witnessed time and again the deliverance from curses, spells, bad luck wishes, death wishes and also healing and miracles that take place. The majority of the people are First Nations people, who at one time or another served and practiced the spiritual beliefs of our parents before they came to Christ. I am sure they must have seen how the medicine men/women are treated. When they come to doctor someone in their family or friends, these medicine men/women are smothered with gifts, offerings and a huge amount of finances. Yet the doctoring that is done by these medicine men/women is not a fully guaranteed healing. To make matters worse they are paid before they even start their vehicles to go to their destination.

My dispute is God's ministers are not treated the same. In my services, the Spirit of God does so many miracles and deliverances. Yet God's ministers get pennies for their work. I am talking through experience. I've been there for both. I did doctoring as a medicine man before I came to Christ. Now I evangelize and do deliverance in the powerful Name of Jesus Christ. Money-wise there is no comparison. Medicine men/women get a huge amount – more than an Indian evangelist could ever get by their own Indian people.

According to the Word of God we Indian ministers for Christ are supposed to be treated like the unsaved treat their spiritual leaders. I have run across some Christians who treated me well, but very far and in between. I was saying to my wife Mary Ann that we as Christians might compare the fact a medicine man/woman who doesn't guarantee a healing to an evangelist who has been called somewhere to preach yet is not guaranteed that he would get anything for his work.

Another huge problem I encountered among our own First Nations people is that they seem to be so unfair when it's time for giving. It seems that they consider their own First Nations brothers less worthy than the White and Black evangelists. They would pile on the financial giving to the White and Black ministers and save the pennies, nickels and dimes for their own First Nations ministers.

For example, there was a ten-day gospel tent meeting held in southern Alberta where I was called to be one of the selected ministers to preach. Each minister had a night to preach. Oh! I tell you every night these White ministers and a couple of Black ministers preached, those offering buckets were full with almost entirely fifty dollar and one hundred dollar bills. They were using KFC barrel chicken buckets – three of them.

It so happened that it was my turn to preach on the last night. To top things off for me, they took the gospel tent down Sunday because they had to set it up somewhere else. If they didn't take it down Sunday, they will be late in the other place.

They moved the last meeting to this huge gymnasium. The place was packed out. When offering time came, they passed a hat around. When it came back, it was full with coins. It seemed they made a mockery out of me and the Lord.

Another time I was called to preach way up in northern Alberta. This was another four days of revival meetings. They had five meetings because they had two meetings on Sunday. They had invited other ministers who were White. About halfway into the four-day revival, there was a huge disagreement among the body of Christians who organized these meetings. I didn't have the slightest idea what this disagreement was about until way after when everything was over.

I guess one brother got upset when he found out that the White minister who was invited also to this meeting was treated differently than I was. I drove my van all the way over there without getting a penny for even gas money. Here the White minister got his round trip plane fare paid, they had hotel room waiting for him, and they got limo service to transport him fifty miles from his hotel to the meeting each night. Here I had to sleep on the road in my van. Nobody even offered me a meal. This was why this disagreement happened.

Another time I was invited to preach. Again I had to travel quite a distance to get there, but I still didn't get any finances for gas from the Christians who invited me.

Like I said earlier, when a medicine man/woman is to be invited to do a doctoring, they travel many miles to seek the medicine man/woman who they choose to do the doctoring. Along with them are gifts and offerings. To top it all off, they bring plenty of finances to guarantee that this person (medicine man/woman) make it to their destination. This should be the case with our First Nations Christian ministers but a very few of them actually do.

I accepted the invitation thinking that I will be rewarded when I get myself there, but I had one big problem. I wasn't employed so I had no income of any kind. I even thought maybe they'll send me some money but that was wishful thinking, because it never happened.

Each day it brought me closer to my invitation and still no finances, when I finally realized if I didn't do anything I was not going to get there. I told my late wife that the only other option that I had left is to start picking empty beer cans and bottles for my gas money. A couple of days before my departure, my late wife drove me a couple of miles out of town. I started walking in the ditch looking for empty cans and bottles. I wasn't in bad shape then, so I walked along the ditch for most of the day and I did real well, not knowing that a lot of the First Nations brothers and sisters in the Lord were passing by on this same highway.

Some later confessed to me on how convicted they felt when they saw me, a chosen vessel of the Lord, picking cans and bottles.

But I am just relaying one of the big problems that we as First Nations Christians have. Because of this, I've always made sure I give above and beyond to ministers that I invite, although it's not very often that I have these meetings. I am always on the road traveling whenever I can.

This is just naming a few of these situations. I could write a whole big book in all the twenty-seven years I've been evangelizing, even right now and before my ailments limited my traveling. My wife and I had to stop ministering, especially our evangelizing, because we weren't getting enough financial support to pay our bills. My wife went back to work to try to catch up to the bills that were piling up.

What I am saying here is it is up to the Christian Indian brothers and sisters to keep their Indian ministers on the road by paying their way, and this is Biblical.75

Jesus Christ himself told His disciples (that's including us ministers) not to carry anything extra, that these needs are supposed to be provided by the people they minister to. When the Indian Christians don't give to their own Indian ministers, many stop evangelizing to their Indian people. Just think how many souls are lost because of this unfair treatment toward their own Indian ministers.

Even when I am not traveling and evangelizing, I am kept busy doing deliverance over the telephone. Sometimes during this time of coasting, I would meet brothers and sister in the Lord while shopping in the city. They would ask me, "Are you still traveling?" I would say, "No, we had to stop. We were not getting the financial support our ministry requires to keep going. We can't live on clap offerings alone, even though the Word of God states:

> *[76]Provide neither gold, nor silver, nor brass in your purses. [10]Nor scrip for your journey, neither two coats, neither shoes, nor staves: for the workman is worthy of his meat.*[77]

Still the Christian Indians won't give to the Christian Indian ministers.

---

[77] Mark 6:7-11

[76]Matthew 10:9, 10

AS FOR ME AND MY HOUSE....[78]

What I noticed when we traveled to many different places was that there were lots of oppression in many of those who needed prayer. These come across different methods and tactics from the devil and the spiritual world.

The devil will use anything and anyone to cause conflict, and he will use something familiar – something that seems harmless. I will use some examples of what we experienced in our travels to show you what I am talking about.

We were visiting in a border city when we were asked to come to pray for a Christian couple's son who was about 12 or 13 years old. This son became very rebellious, defying his parents' wishes and he became angry over even the slightest requests. The parents began to pray with their son and their son repented and he promised to do better. The parents noticed that there was something causing problems even between the man and his wife, and they couldn't understand it. They mistakenly thought their son was going through a "phase" as he was getting older.

When they were cleaning the house one day, the woman asked her husband to pull out the couch. A very small drum was tucked way behind. This drum was only about an inch in diameter, and after asking their son, they discovered that this drum was made in school during cultural week.

These people told us to come over because of their son's behavior, and how the married couple began to argue with each other. As far as the couple knew, they got rid of

[78] Joshua 24:15

everything that didn't honor God. During our conversations, I told them to burn the drum[79], that something that small might seem to be insignificant, but the devil will use anything to cause a rift and to create strife.

We told the parents to explain the Scripture to their son and why the parents believed this way. After burning the drum, their son was not defiant and rebellious. Their son became respectful and obedient once again. This was the son that they knew their son should be.

Things went smoothly for a little while when their son began to act out again. Since the couple knew now what to look for – anything that might be used for Indian cultural ways – they went through their whole house. The bedroom that their son slept in used to be occupied by the woman's sister and her boyfriend who were known to drink and to use drugs. The couple who were Christians took their anointing oil and they prayed over every door and every window and they commanded every evil spirit and evil influence to leave in the Name of Jesus.

There happened to be a loose board in the floor. When the man lifted up the board, he found half of a bottle of whiskey which he poured down the drain.

Another time a few months later, their son began to act out again. We were in town, so we came over. We went into the boy's bedroom and we found all kinds of Yu-gi-O and Pokemon cards. The parents got a garbage bag and we threw the cards, videos, music and pictures that did not honor God. The garbage bag was half full!

After we got back to the Reserve, the couple phoned us to let us know that their son was now content and set free. Praise the Lord!

Teach your children[80]

[79] Deuteronomy 7:25-26

[80] Proverbs 22:6

Sit down with your children and find out what they are doing and how they are thinking and who their friends are. Sharing meals together is a major part of the family unit, and it is very important to know your children. Also invite your children's friends and play games with them. Don't just allow them to come in and go straight to the child's bedroom. It is your job as a parent to make sure their friends are the kind of friends you would approve of.

Another thing that happens throughout Indian Country is that born again Native American Christians don't bring their children to church services. If they do, the children are running around outside and not inside where the service is. The devil will use any kind of influence to bring a wedge between the parents and their children, and to especially cause children to follow after other children who don't know the Lord, or to cause children to fall into temptation.

At many gospel meetings boys will try to gang up on those weaker, and on girls to rape them while the parents are inside praising the Lord. *Know your children* and how they are thinking so that you can correct them and instruct them in the way they should go (Proverbs 22:6).

Put away all evil things

Another time we were preaching the northern Alberta when we were asked to go to a house. This woman wanted us to pray for her nephew because he was so rebellious. He turned up his music real loud, stayed out all hours of the nights and he watched movies that did not honor God. He was out drinking and he wasn't there at the time. We looked in his bedroom and we saw heavy metal music and raunchy videos portraying violence. We told the woman that all of the music and videos had to be burned, as it says in the Word. The woman looked at us and said, "Can't you just pray for him? I can't destroy his property!"

I said, "Whose house is it – yours or his? If you don't get rid of these things, there won't be a change in your nephew." We explained how the influence of music and videos cause rebellion, drinking and all sorts of unwanted behavior in a Christian home.

The woman knew her nephew didn't want to be prayed over, and we couldn't pray effectively for God to intervene with all of the influences still remaining in the household. We prayed for her to have wisdom and to take authority over house[81].

Another time we went to another house with a similar story as above, but this couple had two grown-up sons and one daughter. The sons, too, were drinking and carousing all night and getting in trouble with the law.

Of course, we asked to see their bedroom to see what they were listening to and watching. All over the walls were posters of heavy metal bands and the computer was flashing music videos of other heavy metal bands. It definitely was the devil's playground. My wife started crying because of the influence of the devil upon these grown children.

After coming upstairs we told the parents to clean out their sons' room, and they would not. They wanted their sons to feel comfortable in their home, and the mother was quite upset with my wife. I explained that all of the prayers in the world could not remedy a change in their sons' lives unless the parents would take back authority of what their sons were watching and listening to.

While we were there, we prayed with their daughter who repented and she gave her heart to the Lord. The daughter had an upcoming court date, and the judge ruled in her favor, giving her probation instead of jail time. We also prayed for the parents to take authority, but the struggles continued since they didn't take authority over their house and their sons.

---

[81] Titus 2:15

We prayed for many other people who did throw away and burn music, videos, Indian paraphernalia and cultural relics. Sometimes it seems harmless or too pretty or too valuable, but it is there to cause strife, sickness, bad luck or whatever method the devil uses.

Right in front of our eyes

Even in our own apartment there were items to get rid of – to break into pieces or to burn. My wife saw a black image around a paper box that I brought from Alberta. Inside of the box was a magazine that belonged to someone I used to be romantically attached to. This black image would be in front of, on top of or behind the box and it would flit into the broom closet. Whenever my wife looked out of the corner of her eye, she could see it and then it would disappear. When my wife asked me what was in that box, I told her who it belonged to. When the magazine was torn up and thrown away, all spiritual activity left.

My wife bought a ceramic eagle from a Mexican who set up a stand near her workplace. I was watching TV one night when out of the corner of my eye I saw a black figure hanging around that eagle as if the eagle belonged to it. This happened over and over for about a week, and I told my wife about it. We took it outside and smashed it and we threw it in the dumpster.

The next thing was a magazine rack by the TV stand. This rack belonged to a man who used to use marijuana before he got his life right with God. This man was getting rid of some furniture, and he gave the magazine rack to my wife. Again I saw something like a little grayish-black animal jumping around the rack. We broke up the rack into small pieces and threw it away. That was the end of spiritual activity in our apartment.

My wife is German, and she never was involved with Indian religion or any form of witchcraft. Through these experiences, we both knew that all that is necessary is to open the door to the devil and the evil spirits, and they will infiltrate. At that time we were both born again Christians and going out to preach the Word every chance we got. But because we knew what to look for and how to fight the devil, we were able to get rid of all of these things and live for the Lord in peace and harmony.

One time we stayed at a relative's place, and we were told to sleep in the daughter's bedroom. All over the wall were posters of heavy metal band singers. I told my wife, "How are we supposed to sleep in this bedroom with the devil in here?" My wife took down all of the posters and she set them in the hallway.

The next morning the young girl was upset because the posters were taken down. We explained the influence of these singers that are worshipping the devil, using drugs and the influence of it, and how that would affect her life. We explained that we loved her so much, that we didn't want her to be deceived, and that we wanted her to accept the Lord and to be in Heaven with us someday. She repeated the Sinner's Prayer, but she still wanted her posters back on her wall.

The next time we visited there, the man said that if we were spending the night there, we would have to sleep on the couch and on the twin bed. Being my wife were so close to each other, I tried to sleep on the couch with my wife sleeping on the floor next to me. We couldn't sleep because we felt so much spiritual activity, and we were up most of the night. Both of us laid on the twin bed with our arms around each other, and we prayed for God to protect us, to shield us against the influences of the devil and the evil spirits in that place. In the bedroom where the twin bed was there was a computer that the girl used to listen to heavy metal music. It seemed that we had nowhere to go as long as we stayed in this house.

In the morning after breakfast we left, and we never stayed there again. The man and his girlfriend never got married and later on the daughter and her boyfriend lived together in the girl's bedroom before getting their own place together. My wife found out that the girl's parents bought their daughter birth control pills when the girl was 12 years old so that the parents didn't have to worry about the girl getting pregnant.

My wife was appalled that girl was not taught about abstaining from fleshly desires but that the parents made it easy by giving the girl ways to prevent pregnancy. The boys came in and out of that place, one after another, and never was the girl's bedroom off limits to any boys the girl brought into their home.

If you have a child(ren) or grandchild(ren) – even a young adult(s) – please don't let them walk down the wrong road. It will save them from a lot of heartaches. They will be free from drugs, alcohol and sexual addictions. Too many are having children while they are still children themselves. This is not God's will for His children to experience extreme difficulties – God wants to bless us and our children abundantly[82]. So make the Lord the center of your lives and in your children's lives and may God bless you.

---

[82] John 10:10 – "I am come that they might have life, and that they might have it more abundantly."

CONCLUSION
(WRITTEN BY MARY ANN KOOTENAY)

The above writings were all authored by Adolph Kootenay with the exception of one note that I inserted about his mother. I tried to sort out the stories as best I could. However, everyone's time on this earth has to come to a close, and, Adolph went home to be with the Lord on January 20, 2011, after a long struggle with diabetes and kidney disease.

While we lived on the Alexis Indian Reserve in Alberta, Canada, we spent many hours praying for others and performing deliverance on those who needed to get free from bondage. Many people came from Manitoba, Saskatchewan, Alberta and British Columbia, and we traveled as far south as Florida and as far to the southwest as New Mexico and Arizona. Adolph made a couple of other trips by airplane when I did not accompany him, and every time he went he was proclaiming the gospel to any who would hear.

While Adolph was in dialysis in Bismarck, North Dakota, and in Litchfield and St. Cloud, Minnesota, he talked to all of the nurses, doctors and medical professionals, along with dialysis patients to tell them that we have a God who saves, heals, redeems and that He wants us to give our hearts to Him so that we can live eternally with Him forever.

Adolph lost his right leg below the knee due to gangrene, and he was so brave in learning how to walk with a prosthesis, sometimes falling but always getting up to go on for the Lord. Many, many people were praying for him and me during this time, as we kept the faith, and how we relied on others for strength. Adolph never lost his humor and his love for God and for his family and all of the Christian brothers and sisters. When he spoke to his Christian brothers, he would say, "Brother..."

Adolph was a wonderful man on earth, and I know that he is in his mansion in Heaven and walking the streets of gold and sitting at the feet of Jesus. Our last conversation was: "Adolph, do you want to go home?" and he said, "Yes, I want to go home." And he is home.

ALSO BY ADOLPHUS KOOTENAY,

OUT OF BONDAGE

Out of Bondage describes the path followed by Adolphus Kootenay as he broke from Indian Religion and turned unto the path leading to the Kingdom of God. Because of his keen insight into both worlds, this book will be of great benefit for those who are in Satan's grasp and those seeking ways to release prisoners from Satan's bondage.

In this book Kootenay declares that, "INDIAN RELIGION HAS SIGNS AND WONDERS, BUT NO SALVATION." Kootenay also provides a profound testimony of God's great love. "I WOULDN'T BE HERE WRITING THIS STORY OF HOW JESUS CHRIST SET ME FREE IF HE DIDN'T LOVE THE WICKED. I WAS VERY WICKED."

To order more copies of this book, find books by other Canadian authors, or make inquiries about publishing your own book, contact PageMaster at:

PageMaster Publication Services Inc.
11340-120 Street, Edmonton, AB T5G 0W5
books@pagemaster.ca
780-425-9303

catalogue and e-commerce store
www.ShopPageMaster.ca

ABOUT THE AUTHOR

Adolphus Kootenay, the youngest of five children, was born into the spirit world of his ancestors on July 12, 1945, near the western shores of beautiful Lac Ste. Anne in Alberta, Canada. For more than thirty years Kootenay lived in the spirit world of Indian Religion and for part of that time he practiced as a medicine man, his mother being his mentor. He knows and describes well the traditions of the sweat lodge, the medicine bundle, the peace pipe, and countless ceremonies and rituals. His home and his property were once adorned with offerings and gifts to the spirit world and especially to Mother Earth which he worshipped and honored as a god. Failing health brought Kootenay to his knees in a little church where he accepted Jesus into his heart and began the process of being delivered from Satan's clutches.